THE STORY OF THE NIGHT

By the same Author

THE CHARTED MIRROR: *Literary
and Critical Essays*

THE FUGUE AND SHORTER PIECES
(Poems)

THE
STORY OF
THE NIGHT

Studies in Shakespeare's
Major Tragedies
by
JOHN HOLLOWAY

Routledge & Kegan Paul
LONDON

First published 1961
by Routledge and Kegan Paul Ltd.
Broadway House, 68–74 Carter Lane
London, EC4V 5EL

Second impression 1965
Third impression 1972

Printed in Great Britain
by Fletcher & Son Ltd,
Norwich, Norfolk

© *John Holloway 1961*

ISBN 0 7100 1545 3

To
GEOFFREY L. BICKERSTETH

CONTENTS

ACKNOWLEDGEMENT

MY PRIMARY INDEBTEDNESS in respect of this book is to those earlier critics of Shakespeare, whose writings have demanded study, even though study has issued in dissent. I have also become aware of a long-standing debt, in matters concerning Shakespeare's relation to the ideas of his time, to Mr J. B. Bamborough. I must record indebtedness to a number of colleagues or students, both in Cambridge and elsewhere, for stimulating discussion or telling criticism; and in particular to my wife, Professor Meyer Fortes, and Dr Muriel Bradbrook, for reading and commenting on the manuscript or sections of it. I happily thank all these for their share in any merits this book may have. They have no share in its faults.

Appendix B (p. 166: see the note on p. 187) is reprinted here with acknowledgement to the Colston Research Society, Bristol, and to Messrs. Butterworths Ltd.

Quotations from Shakespeare in this book are based upon the edition of Professor Peter Alexander (1951), and those from the Bible are from an edition of the 'Bishops' Bible' published in London, 1578.

J. H.

Chesterton, Cambridge.

Theseus: Such tricks hath strong imagination . . .
How easy is a bush supposed a bear!

Hippolyta: But all the story of the night told o'er . . .
More witnesseth than fancy's images,
And grows to something of great constancy,
But howsoever strange and admirable.

A Midsummer Night's Dream

I

INTRODUCTION

THERE IS a current coin of Shakespeare criticism. That
statement could be argued and qualified at length: but broadly,
it stands as it is. The facts are doubtless familiar to the reader of
this book; the qualifications are such as he will make for himself;
and no more need be done, than remind him briefly and broadly
of this current coin of criticism, by three quotations from well-
known Shakespeare critics.

The first of these critics is Professor Wilson Knight: 'In
Measure for Measure we have a careful dramatic pattern, a
studied explication of a central theme: the moral nature of man
in relation to the crudity of man's justice.'[1] The second is Mr
Traversi: 'The conceptions elaborated in the new plays [the
writer is speaking mainly of the works to be discussed in the
present book] are indeed more complex than ever before, the
inter-relation of themes even further extended.'[2] The third is
Professor L. C. Knights: who, writing on '*King Lear' and the
Great Tragedies*, refers to Shakespeare's 'attempt to define and
assert certain values' and to his 'obstinate questionings' with
regard to 'all that is most deeply disturbing in human life.'[3]
Mr Bateson has clarified the matter still further. 'A discussion of
tragedy', he writes, 'must begin with what differentiates a good
tragedy from a bad tragedy, the human values embodied and
clarified in it.'[4]

Predilections easily harden into assumptions, and can come
in the end to preclude what they do not include. Some readers

may therefore wonder whether this book, which is not written from the standpoint of the critics who have just been quoted, can possibly discuss matters of importance comparable with those discussed by them; or even, can be criticism at all, in a legitimate or profitable sense. The writer who has such fears for his work might do well to settle for the verdict of Professor L. C. Knights (easily the most modest and engaging of these writers). 'There are other ways of approaching the plays which also make sense', he says in his own most recent book on Shakespeare.[5] Mr Traversi, in issuing a revised edition of his book on Shakespeare, may have had similar ideas, for he changed his title from '*The* Approach to Shakespeare' to '*An* Approach to Shakespeare'. Perhaps I should be wise to avail myself of these concessions.

Certainly it is clear that interests in explicating such themes as the moral nature of man, or in elaborating conceptions, or in obstinately questioning, or in defining, asserting and clarifying values (the omission of 'embodying' will be discussed later) cannot possibly be the only valid approach to the work of a writer of drama. Criticism in terms such as these has become a current coin with remarkably little examination of its fundamentals, of what it does and does not do; partly as a result of denials by certain critics that they themselves are obliged, as critics, to discuss such fundamental questions (which is a not unreasonable claim), and partly through suggestions, quite different in their import, and erroneous, that such questions are intrinsically irrelevant to criticism, and need not be attended to at all. As a result of this, the fact that those interests do not merely happen by chance to be not the only approach to Shakespeare, but cannot possibly be the only approach, seems to have passed unnoticed; and the simple reason why this is so may come as a surprise.

That simple reason is, that when these critics describe Shakespeare's plays in a vocabulary of explicating the moral nature of man, elaborating conceptions, asserting or defining values, and so on, they are not speaking literally. They are speaking in metaphor. It might conceivably be the case, in respect of these plays, that no critical comment whatever was possible unless it was expressed in metaphor. That suggestion, though grotesque, is not absurd. But it simply follows from what a metaphor is, that there is nothing which one metaphor, and one alone, could properly describe.

It is by no means essential to the argument of this book to prove that this vocabulary of explicating, elaborating, questioning, defining and so on is a vocabulary of metaphor. If the present assertion were invalid, the rest would stand perfectly well by itself. Yet that it is a vocabulary of metaphor is plain. Why is this so?

Critics who depend on this vocabulary do not of course confine themselves to metaphorical statements. Thus Professor Wilson Knight quotes a speech from *Measure for Measure*:

Novelty is only in request; and it is as dangerous to be aged in any kind of course, as it is virtuous to be constant in any undertaking. . . .

He asserts that the 'expanded paraphrase', in his view, 'runs thus':

A change (novelty) never gets beyond request, that is, is never actually put in practice. And it is as dangerous to continue indefinitely a worn-out system or order of government, as it is praiseworthy to be constant in any undertaking.[6]

The fact that this assertion is completely wrong, and that Professor Wilson Knight has mistaken a plain and traditional statement of the evils of new-fangledness for something like the opposite of itself, in no way alters the fact that, although completely wrong, what he says is literal and not metaphorical. It is the statements of these critics about explications, conceptions, questionings, definitions, clarifications and assertions which are metaphorical; but these are the nerve of their criticism.

The obvious way to prove that a statement is metaphorical and not literal is to point to something quite other than that of which it is made, and appeal to plain awareness of the idiom of the language to admit that this is what the statement would refer to literally. If a man calls his wife a vixen, and doubts whether this is metaphorical, we produce a female fox. Applied to the claims of these critics, this mode of argument is decisive: though it does not prove that what they say is valueless, only that it is metaphorical. That there are, in standard and idiomatic English, literal uses for all their key terms, and that these uses are quite different from the uses to which they put those terms, cannot be in dispute. In plain English, the definition of a value is a statement of such a kind as 'gratitude is a distinctive kind of emotion, caused by consciousness of more from others than they had an obligation to give'. This is the kind of thing which 'definition', in our language, has as its meaning. It is not an adequate definition of gratitude; but an adequate one would be another form of words of the same kind. Again, the 'clarification' of a value would be something like 'honesty is not only doing what one has undertaken to do, it is also doing what people reasonably expect one to do' (an honest shopkeeper sells only dependable goods, perhaps, but he can hardly be said to have given any undertaking to do so). A 'questioning' means a train of thought which naturally falls into the interrogative mood or one of its equivalents. An explication of the moral nature of man is a piece of discursive prose which in principle could begin, 'The moral nature of man is . . .'. These are the things which these terms mean, when they are used in their literal sense. It would seem odd to commit such banalities to paper, were it not that their import has been overlooked.

As for 'asserting' a value, the expression is barely idiomatic at all, and it ought to disquiet us that it should be used without explanation. If it is said of someone that 'he often asserts values', or that 'he then asserted such and such a value', we should scarcely know what kind of conduct the speaker sought to describe. On reflection, however, something might come to mind. Perhaps, we might think, to assert a value is to say something, at the appropriate stage in a discussion about what course of conduct to pursue, like 'we mustn't disregard sportsmanship': or 'I can't be a party to anything vulgar'. Sportsmanship and the opposite of vulgarity (whatever its name is) are values: and perhaps this is to assert them. Or perhaps, we might feel, to say that someone asserted a value might simply be to stress a certain significance in his conduct rather than his words: he asserted the value of patience (or, patience as a value), simply in remaining patient under trying conditions, or in a conspicuously sustained way, or something of that sort. The expression is a strained and awkward one, but if we reflected along these lines, we should presumably be doing our best with it. Clearly, however, it is to things of these kinds that the expression 'asserting a value' applies literally, if indeed it has any literal use in our idiom at all; and its relation to writing plays is like that of the other terms relied upon by these critics.

Perhaps, at the risk of tedium, the issue ought to be taken one stage further. After all, definitions, questions and the rest may be of more than one kind. Can we be sure that these critics are not merely referring to one kind rather than another, instead of speaking metaphorically and not literally? Yes, and the following illustration suggests why. There are, for example, several kinds of shoes; some fastening with laces, say, some otherwise. If we were told that someone had fastened his shoes, we might infer that he had tied the laces, only to find that on this occasion we had fallen into error, because another kind of shoe was in question. Our experience would be quite different, however, if we were told by someone that he was hunting a vixen, but discovered that what he meant was, he was looking for his wife. In this case, we should think ourselves the victim of a harmless (or perhaps harmless) kind of joke, or a trivial piece of prevarication; and this would be so, because our interlocutor had played a trick on us as between literal and metaphorical meanings. He had so expressed himself as to make us think that he spoke literally. Had he said 'my wife is a vixen', it would have been clear that he was using a metaphor, and the sense of joke, trick or prevarication would have been absent.

Apply this train of thought to the critical vocabulary now under discussion, and the inference is inescapable. Assertions like 'last night I was engaged in obstinately questioning some of the things that are most deeply disturbing in human life', or 'he likes to try his hand at defining values' or 'first he put forward his conception simply, and then he elaborated it', are more or less idiomatic English, and, if we hear them, we form fairly definite expectations. We know that the questions and definitions might take any of several forms, rather as we know that the vixen a man is hunting may be of one or another colour. But if it now transpires that what was meant was, 'last night I writing a play' or 'he likes to try his hand at writing plays' and so on, we shall feel very much as we should feel if the vixen turned out to be a wife. We shall feel that a verbal trick (perhaps a harmless or even an entertaining one) has been played upon us, by way of joke or prevarication. We shall feel, in short, as we regularly do

5

when a metaphorical expression is made to seem like a literal one.

Those who find this discussion intricate and irritating ought to pause before they dismiss it. This is so, because the disadvantages of involving criticism or critics in constant discussion about questions of principle, or fundamental issues which require formulation in general terms, are real enough; but refusal to formulate one's position in such terms, or to discuss questions of principle, has its sinister side also. This is, that such a tactic precludes free enquiry, prevents a free ranging of the mind over the subject. A critic is entitled not to ask himself whether he has expressed his own views in literal or in metaphorical terms (though the concession, set down in black and white, sounds quixotically generous); much as a boxer, say, may reasonably claim that to worry his head about whether he uses his extensor muscles or his weight in a certain punch, makes it harder for him, rather than easier, to deal with particular opponents. Everyone is free to confine himself to what he finds comes easiest, and leave to others what he finds he has no flair for. But for the critic to go further, and pronounce that such a question, by whomsoever handled, has no interest, and no relevance to his work, is for him quite to step out of his province (as it is, be it added, for him in his capacity as critic to dogmatize about the validity of analogies between criticizing and boxing). It is, in effect, for him to seek to insulate his work from scrutiny or questioning at a fundamental level. No reputable critic, we may take it, would knowingly do this.

The purpose of raising this whole issue was to clinch the fact that what was called the current coin of Shakespeare criticism could not possibly be the only profitable kind of criticism. While it was thought (if it was thought) that that current coin consisted of literal statements, it was perhaps possible to think it the only legal tender (*the* 'Approach to Shakespeare'). Once it is seen to consist of metaphorical statements, not only does that possibility disappear, but the wise reader calls to mind what is familiar knowledge about metaphors: that the constant use of one, tends to drive others, also with their utility and their degree of illumination, out of sight. To see the state as organic may bring its distinctive insights, but tends to conceal what would appear plainly, if our paradigm for the state were not an organism but a random aggregate. To see men as animals may throw certain of their qualities into clear relief, but will obscure those which stand out if we think of men as made in the image of God. With this in mind, we shall be so far from wanting to convince ourselves that the current coin of Shakespeare criticism is the only possible one, that we shall wish actively to enquire what aspects of Shakespeare's work this way of discussing it obscures.

Furthermore: we shall begin to entertain a suspicion that in recent years something of a plethora of metaphorical statements about Shakespeare has been created by these critics; so that now, even if only by way of a change, a few literal ones would be much in place;—literal ones, not in the sense of statements about matters of detail, like Professor Wilson Knight's 'expanded paraphrase' (only right, for preference) or about trivial or superficial matters, but literal statements of some kind which were of substantial interest to the critic. If this proved impossible, and the situation were that only trivial critical assertions could be expressed in literal terms, while all the important and interesting ones had to be formulated in metaphor, we should have a situation of the highest oddity and therefore much interest.

One of the purposes of this book is to offer some statements of this kind about the plays which are to be discussed. It is at this point that Mr Bateson's reference to values being 'embodied' in tragedies requires further attention. The expression is of course a common one in current critical parlance; but it is very much in doubt whether all those who use it have sufficiently considered what it can mean (much the same doubt applies to those who rely upon the word 'concrete' to do the same work for them). One may raise the problem, perhaps, by asking whether, if values are both embodied and clarified in dramatic works, the same is true of how they are present in discursive works about values, such as Aristotle's *Ethics*, or Plutarch's *Moralia*, or the essays of Samuel Smiles.

I do not know where to turn for an explicit answer to this question, in the writings of those who make free with the term; and this is perhaps another reflection on their boldness and self-confidence (what could be more grandiosely self-confident than the tone of Mr Bateson's remark quoted above?). But the answer is presumably that discursive works clarify values, but never embody them: this is the characteristic, the distinctive achievement, of the literary or imaginative work. Yet clearly, a Shakespeare tragedy does not embody a value (or values) in the straightforward sense that a building embodies an architect's design. The building *is* the design (or one specimen of it), in concrete form; it is nonsense (or metaphor) to say that the play *is* the value or one specimen of it, in concrete form. Rather, the play embodies its values as the building embodies an architectural value: monumentality, say, or movement, or one of Ruskin's 'Seven Lamps'. The building embodies an architectural value in this sense, however, *as a result of doing something else:* in fact, through embodying, in the other sense, the architect's design. Rather similarly (for the analogy is not a complete one) if a play embodies a value, it will be through embodying, in another sense, something else. What is that something else? It appears to be the action of the play; which may be expressed in summary form ('a king had three daughters . . .'; 'a victorious general met some witches who told him . . .'), but which is embodied in the whole substance of the work.

Today there is a strong tendency to ignore or disparage the mere 'what happens' of a literary work: its plot or narrative or whatever it is called ('O dear yes the novel tells a story':[7] the historical origins of this critical attitude in the practice of a particular creative movement ought to be worked out in full). The present train of thought suggests that this attitude is misjudged; or, to put the matter another way, that when we endorse such a critical principle as that the literary work '*enacts* its moral significance',[8] the word 'enacts' commits us to very much more than seems at first the case. Whether it is the moral significance, or significance of any other kind which interests us, if it is the en*act*ment of this which makes the work a literary and imaginative one, we shall not apprehend that enactment short of apprehending, as fully as we may, the *act*ion of the work taken as a whole; and the action of the work is in some sense the 'what happens' in the course of it. No doubt, there are superficial or tangential ways of describing the 'action' of a literary work, as of describing its moral interest ('*Macbeth* teaches us to distrust our subordinates, *Lear* the opposite'); or of describing anything whatever. If ingenuity has no higher ambition than ineptitude, it is assured of success. But there must also, if what

8

matters about literary works is their being enactments, be another kind of description which is not superficial.

A second purpose of the present book is to offer descriptions of this kind in respect of a number of Shakespeare's tragedies. These will in the first place be literal: but as the discussion proceeds, they will suggest further observations which are metaphorical rather than literal—metaphors buried, it would appear, by the current coin of criticism; and these will have to be scrutinized for their misleading as well as for their illuminating potentialities.

That the critical vocabulary of explicating, defining and so on was a vocabulary of metaphor, was a point made in a particular context which the reader may by now have forgotten. This was, that that vocabulary was not the only one in which literary works might profitably be discussed on the part of the critic. It was pointed out, at the beginning of this chapter, that some critics employing this vocabulary (Professor Knights, and, by implication at least, Mr Traversi) allowed that theirs was simply *an* approach to Shakespeare; and that one might be wise to leave the matter at that, and stake out another territory without finding fault with theirs. This diplomatic course, unfortunately, does not seem quite to suffice. The interest of the new territory does not fully emerge, unless attention is drawn to what is wrong with the old.

Today, there seems to be a widespread view that the good critic 'just criticizes'. He brings a trained and disciplined sensibility to bear on the work, and (although, certainly, this means bringing his total sense of life and sense of value to bear) the instrument of critical judgement is simply that 'sensibility': the critic's response is the direct verdict of that. This is a delusion; and those who speak as if it were the truth merely foster the obscurantism which insulates criticism from itself being scrutinized at a fundamental level, a level where the critic's whole approach, not only his findings, comes under review. A critic's response is seldom of that primaeval and undifferentiated kind. A trained and disciplined sensibility is not merely a sharpened sensibility: it is an equipped one. The formed and disciplined critic tends to ask the same questions about one work after another; to find, recurrently, similar grounds for praise or condemnation; and to a greater or lesser extent, to record his findings in a recurrent terminology: of which the terminology of the critics now being discussed is an example.

To the degree that a critic (or a number of critics) repeatedly asks the same question of the works he discusses, repeatedly brings forward similar findings as matters of prime interest, and repeatedly does so in the same vocabulary, there is, implicit in what he writes, a more or less definite idea of the *real nature of a literary work*. There is an 'ulterior conception' of what a work must be *to be literature*. The critic may not have formulated this idea explicitly to himself. He may even be the better critic for not doing so. For all that, it is there, and it controls what he does. Sometimes his criticism may unconsciously divagate from his usual 'ulterior conception'; and sometimes, perhaps, this may be not for the worse but for the better, rather as an artist may surpass himself in a half-intended and uncharacteristic work. But in the critic's writing taken by and large, there is that implicit idea; and the vocabulary he is steadily content to use, the questions that he regularly raises, are among our chief clues to it.

Fully to define the 'idea of a work' implicit in any body of criticism would be a major task. But if we review the vocabulary of the body of criticism which has been discussed in this chapter —a vocabulary of explicating such themes as the moral nature of man, of asking questions, elaborating conceptions, defining and clarifying values and so on—and still more if we add to these, some of the other terms in regular use by these critics and others associated with them, terms like 'problem', 'significance', 'discrimination', 'insight', 'evaluation'—something about the implicit idea is obvious. It is, that the thing which gives a work interest and value, makes it 'literature' in the full sense, is some kind of *informativeness*. Not, of course, mere informativeness on such matters as which characters do which things, or the like; but informativeness of a more general kind, informativeness which bears generally and substantially on the lives of men. Here one must speak with circumspection. No one suggests that the literary work offers its informativeness in a plainly discursive manner. If it generalizes, it does so implicitly, through the medium of the concrete situations it depicts. Probably even this caveat does not fully represent the idea behind the work of these critics. Each of them suggests that the informativeness of the works they are concerned with, though relevant somehow generally to life, represents a kind of knowledge different in essential quality from that which can be embodied in general statements, however these are elaborated. The insight offered by the literary work is not, they might insist, reducible to any abstract formulation whatever, not even in principle. Clearly, it is not unconnected with knowledge such as may be so expressed; for one critic after another, when he comes to define what he calls the 'theme' of the work he is examining, sets down something which in effect *is* a general statement about human life or some part of it; and it is surprising how terse these themes can be, and how trite and partial, usually, are the items of knowledge about life which they offer. For all that, we must keep in mind that the informativeness of the literary work, as envisaged by these critics, is other than, and no doubt richer than, anything which generalizations could pin down.

The full story of how this 'ulterior conception' has become influential, and especially influential in recent decades, would be a major piece of research into cultural history. One part of that story may be that we have been living through a time when literature has had to face a challenge from science and the social sciences. The sciences are nothing if not informative, and perhaps the defenders of literature have defended it in the image of what they thought threatened it. Another may be that over the past few decades it has seemed especially important to many concerned with literature to emphasize the contrast between treating books merely as idle entertainment, and treating them as making a profoundly serious contribution to life; and this contrast has very much invited being made by the assertion that the best literature has a *meaning*, which constitutes that important contribution. A third may be that the trend of criticism now being considered has grown up among teacher-critics, and it is natural enough for a teacher to see value as informativeness. A fourth, perhaps, is that at least from the time of Matthew Arnold, literature has been especially (and in a way very different from the other arts) thought of as offering help to people perplexed over 'how to live'; and it seems as if such help would naturally take the form of guidance over questions about living which had perplexed them.

Influential as these forces may have been, however, I must admit that the results of them leave me in difficulties. A teacher like other writers of books about Shakespeare—and I should be sorry to seem supercilious in regard to them: no academic writer advances on the work of his colleagues, save because he has had the privilege of reflecting on what they have said in fields where they trod first—I am always glad to see a good word spoken for instruction; and since a teacher is always a learner, to acquire a little for myself, especially about morality, which (as I find in Matthew Arnold) is three fourths of life. Shakespeare has seemed to me an incomparable dramatist ever since I read the others; and as it therefore follows from Mr Bateson's dictum that he is an incomparable clarifier of values, I turn, with the highest hopes, to those who have written about this side of his work. Imagine my discomfiture, to find that this incomparable clarity demands elucidation in prose as clotted as Mr Traversi's, as inconclusive (often enough) as Professor Knights', as febrile as Professor Knight's! Why must what Shakespeare defined be re-defined like this? This is to carry not coals, but ash, to Newcastle.

Nor are my difficulties over. I make it a first principle in studying Shakespeare to bear in mind that his was a more capacious mind than my own. When, therefore, critics give accounts of Shakespeare's explicating and defining which would convict him of being less well informed about life even than I am myself, I am obliged to infer that they are casting not light but darkness. Professor Enright says:

The theme of [*Coriolanus*] . . . seems to me . . . the dangers that are often implied in the word 'political'—the dangers of a situation in which each opposing side understands the other . . . but neither side understands itself.[9]

Fettered as I am by my admiration for Shakespeare, I call certain simple facts to mind, and cannot possibly attribute this to his play. To understand the opposing side well, and one's own side ill, is not what generally holds of political situations, is a common feature of situations which are in no sense political, and is almost unrelated to the moral dangers to which those in politics are by the nature of things exposed.

Again, Professor Bithell stated that:

In *Antony and Cleopatra*, Shakespeare returns to the old problem: what are the positive bases of the good life? He finds them in the affections, and in the affections as rooted deep in the sensual nature.[10]

I ask myself, could Shakespeare have been so confused and ill-informed about life as this? The idea is absurd: yet not more so, than to fail to know that the positive bases of the good life must at the most be 'rooted' only in part in the affections, and that out of the many kinds of affection which have a part in the good life, it is very doubtful whether more than one should have any roots whatever in the sensual nature.

Again, Professor Knights claims that the supreme value asserted by *King Lear* is a distinctive kind of love: that which is, among other things, 'the condition of intellectual clarity'.[11] Well, Shakespeare was not divine; he may have erred; but could he have erred as badly as that? It is simply not the case (unless we define our terms so as to beg the question: and here, even this would be a *tour de force*) that love is the condition of intellectual clarity. If this were part of the play's assertion, the play would be the worse for it.

All these difficulties arise for me simply through my great admiration for Shakespeare; but the chief difficulty is still to come. It is, that if I am to believe all these writers say, Shakespeare turns out not only to have had a limited understanding of life and an unfortunate proneness to assertions, definitions and clarifications in which confusion and error play major and complementary rôles; worse than this, he proves to have suffered from some kind of deep-seated moral irresponsibility, something amounting almost to a radical moral disorder. The study of literature, to be sure, is a bracing discipline; but I scarcely saw, when I turned to it, that it would administer such shocks as this.

The early seventeenth century was a notable period of moral and religious thinking in England; and many of its chief convictions in these fields had deep roots and a deep justification in the whole civilization of that time, and what it demanded of its members in the sphere of conduct. Today, in our very different civilization, some of these convictions have been displaced, I think, from the centre of our moral needs and our moral consciousness; but as we encounter them in the writing of that period, we cannot fail to admire their unflinching and uncompromising confrontation of the conditions of men's life then, and the demands, stern though these might be, which life then made. Yet to judge by the critics whose work is now under discussion, Shakespeare seems barely to have been conscious of these nodal points in contemporary morality. The peculiar heinousness of usurpation; the controversial obligation to avenge one's forbears; the duties of unquestioning obedience and submissiveness within the family—child to parent, wife to husband, sister to brother;[12] the duty of those in great place to live publicly and conspicuously up to their place, and of those beneath them to defer to and revere them; the fact that illicit sexual intercourse might be filthy, degrading and inhuman—these ideas, it would seem, barely play a part in the moral life of Shakespeare's dramas. Nor do other central convictions of the time, of a kind where the moral consciousness verged upon the religious. Among these, come such ideas as that life on earth was a place of trial and a vale of tears, towards which an attitude of repudiation at the deepest level was an acceptable part of the Christian life, especially in preparation for death;[13] and that the evil-doer, so far from being redeemed ('all the major evil characters of [*King Lear*] die into love', writes Professor Knight), might be punished in this world or the next with suffering calculatedly and vindictively matching to his evil deeds, though perhaps immeasurably outweighing them.

Of these ideas, stern, coherent and splendid as (in relation always to their time) they clearly are, Shakespeare, to judge by accounts, was unconscious. Not that he was a moral idiot. He grasped, sure enough, the fundamental notions which (none the worse for being truisms) are the basis of acceptable morality in any society. But of how these had been viably worked out in his own age he was almost wholly innocent. Instead, he had developed an elaborate, though irrelevant, morality of his own. Here it is inevitable that, in order to make the point which now has to be made, I should notice certain recurrent trends and tendencies in the work of these critics, rather at the expense of noticing the things which most distinguish them one from another. But if this is allowed, one may say (some of the details emerge in later chapters of this book) that the morality which they tend to see in Shakespeare was one which paid little regard to the evil of usurpation, or to either the duties or the claims of those in a great station of life; for it viewed public affairs in general with distaste, as making life crude and corrupting its finer values. Violence it found repulsive (to judge by some of

14

these critics), 'reason' it found (to judge by Professor Knight) abstract, futile and even evil. Military prowess was boring and irrelevant, public renown and honour, empty and a trifle ridiculous. What it took its stand by were what Professor Enright termed, in a comprehensive gesture, 'life'.[14] Shakespeare was 'for life'; and life was something in which for example voluptuousness was not a violent and intensely real temptation so much as an improbable posture, 'senseless' or 'self-dramatizing'; and love had little to do with self-effacing dutifulness on the one hand, and the just use of rightful authority on the other, but (particularly for Professor Knight) was private, idealistic and a good deal emotionalized.

All this is unfortunate, surely, and even embarrassing: for if Shakespeare, in the early seventeenth century, held these views, he was not only gravely deficient in moral insight, but he had only the universal impercipience of his contemporaries to thank for not suffering as a destructive and dangerous moral firebrand. Not, of course, that this would be true of such views in all periods. In the very different social, political, domestic and hygienic conditions of our own time, for example, these convictions would be far from unacceptable. Indeed, they are not uncommon today; and in part (though only in part) I should endorse them myself. Many teachers of English would find them much more sympathetic: in fact, would endorse them warmly and *in toto*. A new image of Shakespeare begins to take shape; unfortunately the images of various kinds of twentieth-century don are insufficiently remote from it.

The dilemma is no trifle. On the one hand, one can decide that Shakespeare's sense of value was, to begin with, often confused in formulation and badly tangled with simple errors of fact about life; and more than that, almost wholly unrelated to the needs of his time; and more than that again, intrinsically defective in its escapism (partial repudiation of public life) and lack of fibre (reliance on an emotional idea of love as panacea). On the other hand, one must suppose that the writings of these critics has often been undisciplined and irresponsible; that they have in effect made use of Shakespeare for preaching of their own, writing of his work but venting their personal moralities. Of these repulsive alternatives, I find the former (though not by much) the more repulsive. I still retain my conviction of

Shakespeare's incomparable merits; and besides this, I detect something disquieting in the fact that these writers on Shakespeare as explicator, definer and clarifier of values never even hint that his views are wrong, or partly wrong, or applicable to our own age and its quite different conditions of life only with qualification. This implies either very great impercipience; or an indifference to moral questions which is not to be associated with their work; or some re-making of Shakespeare in their own image. But the findings to which this points are unattractive, and I prefer not to pursue them.

The more so, because it is high time to come to something else. The difficulties which have been discussed in the last few pages relate only to how the 'ulterior conception' of the literary work as above all a fount of informativeness (in particular, moral informativeness) has been worked out by a particular group of critics. If the upshot is that those who have taken their stand by that conception have fared very ill, that affords a kind of *prima facie* argument against the idea itself, but it does not argue against it conclusively. There is, however, a radical objection to this as an adequate idea of what essentially gives a great work of literature its great merit. This objection, if valid, still does not demonstrate that the great work carries *no* informativeness about life. That view would be absurd. A writer engaged upon a great work draws upon all his resources. His powers for imparting information about values, or what gives life meaning, or simply how it is lived, are part of those total resources; and draw upon those powers, along with all his others, he undoubtedly will. What follows is only an argument against the view that such informativeness is the essence of what makes great works of literature valuable: what, that is, makes them great.

This matter may be put simply. The essence of the 'ulterior conception' of a work of literature which is under discussion, is that it is a certain kind of statement; uniquely rich, uniquely complex, but a statement none the less. If this idea is reflected upon, it becomes clear that our response to a great work of art is different in kind from our response to the sort of statements which, it is alleged, such works make; and that the place of great works of literature in the cultures to which they belong is also different in kind from the place of such statements as are in question. There is a radical disparity and divergence which sets it beyond doubt that the essences of these two things are different.

Prominently within the response of the appreciative reader, or spectator, to a great work of literature, comes an intense and varied play of emotion; prominent among these emotions come feelings of tension or concern on the one hand, and of delight, relief or admiration on the other. The outcome of reading (or watching) the whole work may indeed be that we are left with many new ideas about what life is like or may be like, and that our own perception of life may prove to have been made larger and keener in many directions. But there is also a quite distinctive emotional condition in which most (not, I think, all) great works leave us. It is a condition at once exuberant and reposed: the sense of having passed through a great experience, one which testifies (as do great experiences of any kind) to the superb wealth and range of life, and to the splendid rather than the disastrous powers of man.

The place which great works of literature have, in the societies which possess and enjoy them, is likewise that they permanently offer, and invite, such responses as these. They are precious to those societies as inexhaustible sources of delight, energy and exuberance. Needless to say, great imaginative works, like every other great thing, are many-sided, and do many things at once. But along with a society's other forms of great art it is this which they do characteristically and super-abundantly. Many other forms of writing, and many traditions of education in family, school and elsewhere, contribute to our insight into value as into other matters, and transfer that insight from generation to generation. But before it is a source of insight, great imaginative literature is a source of *power*.

There may be certain insights, certain 'statements', which carry some measure of this varied emotional excitement, this exuberant repose, and this sense of life-giving energy. 'I am Saved' may, for some people, be one. 'The Revolution has succeeded', 'We love each other', 'the war is won' suggest themselves, conceivably, as others. But it is clear that no one thinks of great literary works as conveying insights even remotely like these; and the matter need not be pursued further, save to notice that the emotional and vitalizing power of these statements is inseparable from their promising, or more probably accompanying, what is altogether outstanding in the hearer's life *as experience*.

No one can suppose that any moral insight, however rich and complex, invites this sort of response. When we learn that such and such a value is one of the supreme values of life, or such and such an evil one of the supreme evils, or receive any other kind of moral insight, our response is one of serious and interested attention combined with gladness for valuable knowledge; and it perhaps includes also an immediate desire to behave in conformity with the insight (though that desire will probably have the muted quality of a merely contingent desire, in that circumstances in which we come by a moral insight, and at the same moment are given an opportunity of putting it into practice, are rare). The more richly and completely the insight is proffered to us, the greater must be our concentration, and will therefore be our sense of mental effort; and the stronger, perhaps, will be the other responses which have just been mentioned. But it is self-evident that our response to a great work of literature is of an altogether different kind. Thoughtful and interested attention, thankfulness for valuable knowledge, a desire to do this or that may be present, but are all peripheral. It is no good for the champions of the conception of the great work as a unique kind of statement to say that the difference is constituted by the insights being asserted 'concretely'. To intensify, elaborate or deepen a response of one kind will never turn it into one of a wholly different kind. Arguing like that is the same as saying that the water in a river is a function of its length, breadth and depth: to measure the first two is easy, and for the third you must gaze right into the river; once you have seen into it to the bottom, then you sense its full content. This will suffice only for lakes. For rivers, there is something else (viz., the current, the power moving) to take into account: no depth in a lake will turn it into a river however shallow. The issue here is similar. Perhaps one could put it another way. If it is the concreteness of the work that counts in making it what it is—its depiction of human situations and emotion, its enactment of a great event from beginning through to end—that concreteness is not what simply gives the moral insight of the work its full measure of impact. It is what goes immeasurably beyond that.

It is what brings a comprehensive excitement of the whole gamut of emotion, a general sharpening and broadening of all our powers of perception, and a joyous re-vitalization which operates at a profound level on the whole personality. To try to express all these things in a vocabulary of expressing moral insights 'concretely' is at bottom to deprive words of their meanings.

Yet great works of literature (or indeed, of art in general) are not unique in having this kind of impact; or at least, there is a partial parallel to it, as the impact of the moral statement, however enriched, is no parallel at all. This parallel has already been mentioned, in connection with those statements which seemed to have a quite special order of power in inducing our response to them ('I am Saved' and the like). The parallel is, the *outstanding and momentous experience*. Examples, which must of necessity draw intimately on the lives of those who give them, are unnecessary. Nearly everyone has had experiences which have invited and demanded an intense and varied play of emotion, a general heightening of all the powers of apprehension and a great access of life-giving energy. Here is the direction in which the discussion must turn.

The examination of a number of Shakespeare's plays which follows has its 'ulterior conception' of the great work of art, its own paradigm and guide, just like the examinations which have been scrutinized in this preliminary chapter. But I do not wish to have it left undiscussed: I should prefer to force it upon the attention. It is, that such a work is not a statement or insight or special kind of informativeness—not these things essentially, though it may be all of them incidentally—but is a *momentous and energizing experience*. The major aspect of what makes the dramatic (or non-dramatic) *fiction* such an experience has already been indicated. It is the whole action, the whole developing course that it pursues from the beginning of the work to the end. So far, what has been said is asserted literally. But at an earlier stage in this chapter, it was suggested that the vocabulary of metaphors (question, problem, explication, assertion, definition and the rest) used by the moralist-critics of Shakespeare, perhaps averted our gaze from other metaphors which might in their turn throw light on the plays. In the closing chapters of this book it will be suggested that a new guiding metaphor emerges quite naturally from a careful review of these works; and an attempt will be made to delineate the powerful, if doubtless partial, light that it sheds.

In conclusion, something must briefly be said of one objection which might be brought against this book as a whole: that it is not sufficiently critical in the sense of arguing constantly towards a relative *evaluation* of the works it discusses. It ought in the first place to be noticed that this is generally the case, and for fairly obvious reasons, with work on Shakespeare's major plays, even by those most ready to insist on the need for criticism to make judgements of value. Besides this, it might be added that the critical judgements which would emerge if the ideas of this book were pressed in that direction, are plain enough, and some of them appear in the closing chapter. But the real reasons why this book does not force value-judgements on the reader are that the plays, widely misunderstood, are still much in need of discussion which puts the stress on interpretation. This is so, not to enlighten the ignorance of centuries, but to restore traditional clarity by removing modernistic over-ingenuity. Moreover, when this is done, a problem seems to arise about the common nature of the plays, insofar as they have one. These matters are enough for one book.

II

'HAMLET'

THE CURRENT COIN of Shakespeare criticism condemns, as is well known, an approach to the plays through Bradleian 'character-analysis' (though the critics of this school are not above ingenious interpretations of character themselves when it suits their purpose). There is, however, a reason for not attempting to probe the character of Hamlet, besides those which argue in general against this approach to the plays. It is, that by contrast with what is often thought, the *character* of this character (if one may so put it) is not displayed to us with unusual fulness; and we are not even afforded good reasons for supposing it to be abnormally intricate. Undoubtedly, Hamlet displays an *intelligence* which is perhaps unsurpassed in drama for its fertility and intricacy. That is another matter. Again, his consciousness, the whole working of his mind, is undoubtedly presented to us throughout the play with unequalled fulness and detail. But character is not intelligence, and it is not consciousness.

If one wishes to investigate Hamlet's character, there is of course much to build upon; but since he is often shamming and sometimes a good deal distracted, there is little cause for surprise if that evidence is built upon with difficulty. Indeed, an important general point emerges. No doubt a character in a great play must be a vivid presence. No doubt also his nature must be such that what he does and suffers can issue convincingly from what he is, and be imposed convincingly upon it. But no play has to be seen as an illustration, articulate in every

21

detail, of all-pervading causality, of character issuing, at every point, systematically into action. Perhaps this is a characteristically nineteenth-century way of seeing drama, as indeed it was in that time a new and exciting discovery about how to see life. But in essence, a great dramatic spectacle does not require its audience to form an exact view, in all detail, of the 'characters' of all the major characters. Its momentum is drawn from other and more distinctively dramatic sources.

The present discussion does not begin by raising the matter of Hamlet's character. Yet there is a fact about this play as about its author's other tragedies, which is so prominent that it ought to be given recognition. It is this. In nearly all of Shakespeare's major tragedies the hero, the protagonist, has a very great and indeed a peculiar prominence. There is no parallel to this in Shakespeare's other plays, not even the most tense and serious of them, like *Measure for Measure* (in its early scenes) or *The Winter's Tale*. Nor is it paralleled in all tragedies by other authors (the contrast with most of Racine's plays, or *The Trojan Women* of Euripides, is plain). But for all that, this prominence is not rightly seen in terms simply of character.

It is rather, that we make contact very directly with the *experience* through which the protagonist passes in the course of the play. The issue is not, what kind of man Hamlet *is*; but what he *does*. Or rather, what he both does and undergoes: how one can describe the whole volume of the experience through which he passes, as one who both acts and suffers the action of others. Because of the peculiar prominence of the protagonist, to see lucidly what he has experienced, in this sense, will in large part be to see our own experience as spectator. By no means, of course, will it be wholly to see this. The spectator enters into the experience of the protagonist; he also stands back from it. But to have diagnosed the experience through which that peculiarly prominent character passes is to have made a start with taking stock of the experience of the spectator himself.

Hamlet's experience in the course of the play does not take him from the top of Fortune's Wheel to the bottom. This would express the facts only crudely and misleadingly. At the beginning, everyone's interest and concern and loyalty is ostensibly (and often truly) centred upon him. All the characters in the first scene turn at the end of it to him as the man to deal with their crisis and the man to whom they are devoted:

> *Hor:* Let us impart what we have seen to-night
> Unto young Hamlet; for, upon my life,
> This spirit, dumb to us, will speak to him.
> Do you consent we shall acquaint him with it,
> As needful in our loves, fitting our duty?
>
> (I. i. 169–73)

In the scene which follows, Claudius and the Queen, as soon as the necessary business has been disposed of (it is plain that the order of events could not have been reversed, save at the expense of disastrous bathos) both give Hamlet the central place in their thought and their court, make him the cynosure of Denmark, and solicit him to accept this kind of position within the society of which they are the heads:

> *King:* We pray you throw to earth
> This unprevailing woe, and think of us
> As of a father; for let the world take note
> You are the most immediate to our throne;
> And with no less nobility of love
> Than that which dearest father bears his son
> Do I impart toward you. For your intent
> In going back to school in Wittenberg,
> It is most retrograde to our desire;
> And we beseech you bend you to remain
> Here, in the cheer and comfort of our eye,
> Our chiefest courtier, cousin, and our son.
> *Queen:* Let not thy mother lose her prayers, Hamlet:
> I pray thee stay with us; go not to Wittenberg.
> *Hamlet:* I shall in all my best obey you, madam.
> *King:* Why, 'tis a loving and a fair reply.
> Be as ourself in Denmark.
>
> (I. ii. 106–22)

The King's words bring to notice an important dramatic principle. To see them as helping to build up the King's character is to give them the wrong kind of weight. That Claudius has at first a fund of genuine benevolence towards Hamlet, or that from the start he is afraid, and full of eagerness to placate and disarm potential opponents, would be facts (if facts they were) of only secondary importance. But in Shakespeare,

where there is no dramatic chorus, the characters speak con-
tinually, not perhaps out of character (though sometimes they
do even this), but independent of their character, as a kind
of running implicit chorus. Their words clarify the situation to
the spectator. This is the primary function of what Claudius
says here. It shows Hamlet's central position.

Each new scene, at the beginning of the play, underlines the
same idea. Act I scene ii shows Ophelia in love with Hamlet,
and her brother preoccupied with him. In scene iv Hamlet is the
only man to whom the ghost will speak. Early in Act II,
Polonius and the King are still preoccupied, and on the face of
it benevolently so, with Hamlet's affairs and with his welfare.
Rosenkranz and Guildenstern are to give him their company and
'draw him on to pleasures'. This is Hamlet's central and especially privileged position as the play opens. He is still what
Ophelia calls him a little later when she thinks of the past:

> Th'expectancy and rose of the fair state,
> The glass of fashion and the mould of form,
> Th'observ'd of all observers
>
> (III. i. 152–4)

Yet, save for the very first scene, this universal deference is
real only within limits. It may not be feigned, but there is something ceremonial in it, there is a nuance of withholding the
reality of being a central figure. Claudius's concern is real, but
even before Hamlet's closing soliloquy, it is clear that the
King's motives are not often unmixed. Laertes' preoccupation
is also an alienation. Ophelia may love Hamlet, but she aban-
dons him. Polonius at the end of Act II scene i might be said
still to be a friend:

> I am sorry that with better heed and judgment
> I had not quoted him. I fear'd he did but trifle,
> And meant to wreck thee; but beshrew my jealousy!
> By heaven, it is as proper to our age
> To cast beyond ourselves in our opinions
> As it is common for the younger sort
> To lack discretion. Come, go we to the King.
> This must be known.
>
> (II. i. 111–18)

Even so, he is soon trying to pick Hamlet's brain for the benefit of the King and Queen behind the arras. As for Rosenkranz and Guildenstern, Hamlet constantly wishes to call them 'friends', and does so over and over; but their friendship, real enough in the past (II. i. 20–1), is now a façade. When Guildenstern has heard the King's request to sound Hamlet, and replies:

> Heavens make our presence and our *practices*
> Pleasant and helpful to him!
>
> (II. ii. 38–9)

the italicized word comes with the full Machiavellian ring of its Elizabethan meaning.[15] It is not long before Hamlet realizes that he can trust these 'old schoolfellows' only as 'adders fanged' (III. iv. 203).

Indeed, as the play progresses, Hamlet is placed more and more in a characteristic relation: his fellows surround him with their attentiveness, offer him their conversation and concern ('They fool me to the top of my bent', III. ii. 372). But it is a façade more like a strange kind of baiting than genuine concern; and the note of harshness, of force to be used on the invalid or the victim if all else fails, is always present and if anything it grows. With Claudius's soliloquy (IV. iii. 58–68) revealing his scheme for Hamlet's assassination in England, with the murderous duel plotted by Claudius and Laertes (IV. vii), and more particularly with the graveyard scene when Laertes seizes Hamlet by the throat and says:

> The devil take thy soul
>
> (V. i. 253)

—with these, the covert hostility to Hamlet comes out into the open. Hamlet's response relates this incident to how Ophelia, Rosenkranz, Guildenstern and indeed his mother (who also tried to sound him for the benefit of a hidden listener) have all gone over to the other side. It is the response of a man who thought mistakenly that he had a friend:

> Hear you, sir:
> What is the reason that you use me thus?
> I lov'd you ever. But it is no matter.
>
> (V. i. 282–4)

Finally—in what is almost a symbolic moment, so brief it is and yet so significantly placed—Hamlet parts company with

Horatio, rejecting his advice to avoid the duel; Horatio with whom, as with Rosenkranz and Guildenstern, he once rejected any title but that of friend (II. ii. 221-3; I. ii. 162-3). Horatio does not speak again until after the lethal blows have been struck; and apart from him, in this crucial scene Hamlet acts in the conspicuous isolation of one who fights in single combat surrounded by those who in one way or another are on the side of the opponent.

This distinguished isolation is aptly expressed in the likeness which the play often throws out for Hamlet: the lonely moon, the single star. As illustrations of this one may count Laertes' 'The chariest maid is prodigal enough / If she unmask her beauty to the moon' (I. iii. 37); Hamlet's own reference, which applies ironically to himself, to 'Nature's livery or fortune's star' (I. iv. 32); his letter to Ophelia—'Doubt thou the stars are fire . . . but never doubt I love' (II. ii. 115); and perhaps, in view of its ironical reference back to his own honesty in a world of intrigue, his words to Laertes before the duel: 'I'll be your foil, Laertes: in mine ignorance / Your skill shall like a star i' th' darkest night, / Stick fiery off indeed' (V. ii. 247). The contribution of the imagery is not prominent, but it is there. Yet the whole action of the work progressively bringing out Hamlet's position in its starkest truth, carries—as it should—the main weight.

A part of Hamlet's experience, over the play, is to pass from one of these extreme positions to the other: from centrality to isolation. His experience has that shape, and that measure of integration: and ours has the reflection of it as we watch. As for Hamlet's character, the experience is related less to that than to what overrides it and renders it irrelevant. In this play as in many other tragedies, the experience of the protagonist is not the deployment of a determinate character, but the assumption, and then the enactment, of a determinate *rôle*. Rôle predominates over character, because once it is assumed by an actor, it will be much the same whatever his nature may be. It overrides that nature: the play is its acting out.

At least twice, Hamlet refers explicitly to his having taken on (albeit unwillingly) the task of the revenger whose narrower function may have been to avenge a wronged kinsman, but whose wider one was to purge from society the evil which it could not otherwise escape.

The time is out of joint. O cursed spite,
That ever I was born to set it right!
(I. v. 189–90)

and

For this same lord
I do repent; but Heaven hath pleas'd it so,
To punish me with this, and this with me,
That I must be their scourge and minister.
(III. iv. 173–5)

—both these quotations express the sense on Hamlet's part that
he is discharging a rôle; one which, so far from being a product
of character, is something thrust upon that. Much in the play
confirms this. The scene at the close of Act I scene v is a
deliberate self-dedication, made as conspicuous as possible, to
the rôle of a revenger. Hamlet invents a brief ritual, a ceremony,
the grimly humorous writing of Claudius down in his tablets;
and he follows this with the more conventional ceremony of
swearing the others to be his confederates. The whole, as will be
seen later, has striking parallels in other plays; its function is to
make both conspicuous and solemn the moment when Hamlet
took upon himself the rôle which henceforth he is to act and
suffer.

Much else in his part would have had this recognizable and
conventional quality for the spectator of the time, though
scholarship has now to recover it. This is true of his cynicism
about chastity in women, and about cosmetics; of his passing
references to his own ambition; of his other conventional or
traditional musings, for example on the *de contemptu mundi* theme,
on the arguments for and against suicide and (following
Castiglione) on how and when the honourable man may engage
in violence.[16] The same also applies to his variations of *loci
classici* in Seneca's tragedies: ('I have that within which passeth
show', I. ii. 85: 'Curae leves loquuntur, ingentes stupent',
Hippolytus, 607; 'I shall win at the odds. But thou wouldst not
think how ill all's here about my heart; but it is no matter . . .
not a whit, we defy augury', V. ii. 203–10: 'Nihil timendum
video, sed timeo tamen,' *Thyestes*, 435). These details all point
the same way.

To take them, however, as indications of character (that
Hamlet, say, had a tendency to slip into conventionalities in

moments of stress) would be ludicrous; to take any of them (say, those about unchastity or honour) as seriously entering the fabric of ideas of the play would not be ludicrous but would be to seek the far-fetched at the expense of the obvious and central. What is central is the recognizable rôle which has been assumed, the situation (familiar in a general way in the very idea of the revenge play and the malcontent) which is progressing phase by phase before our eyes. These details keep those central facts steadily before our attention; they remind constantly of what the events are that have arrested us. We have a recognizable kind of situation, a man engaged in a known career.

With this in mind, Hamlet's soliloquies take on a new appearance. One must bear in mind that they are, after all, easily foremost in bringing the idea of his delay to notice. It is meaningless to see a delay, in a fiction, merely because something that requires doing is not done at once. The story is of its doing. Naturally it will be done at the end of the story, if it is what will end it. A reader or spectator may see procrastination only if the fiction underlines procrastination. In Saxo Grammaticus's account of Hamlet's taking revenge, mere length of time counts for nothing. Hamlet makes his journey to England (which he does not reach at all, of course, in Shakespeare), stays there a whole year, and at the end of the time merely returns 'thirsting to exact the vengeance, *now long overdue*, for his father's murder'.[17] The author does not raise the question of why it was overdue, and it does not raise itself.

In the play, and apart from the soliloquies, the idea that Hamlet delays can be traced only to two passages. The first is the single occasion when we see him reject a real opportunity for the King's death (the latter is praying after the play scene). No weight can be given to this, for what it mainly does is to give a striking theatrical twist: Hamlet seems to have a fine chance to put an end to his own self-anger at delaying; and then, when he thinks twice, it seems to prove no chance at all. The second passage also deserves little stress, for it is merely that the Ghost (III. iv. 110–11) endorses Hamlet's own suggestions that he has come, his 'tardy son to chide'. Were it not for Hamlet's own soliloquies, whether he delayed or not would barely invite notice.

It is now possible, however, to see the stress on delay in the soliloquies as being not so much for the sake of stressing delay itself, as of showing how the protagonist is preoccupied with his rôle, in order to stress that it *is* a rôle: a recognizable 'part', undertaken by him with what might almost be termed a preordained course and end. This is in fact constantly the burden of the soliloquies. 'But break, my heart, for I must hold my tongue' (I. ii. 159); 'from the tablet of my memory / I'll wipe away all trivial fond records' (II. v. 99). 'What would he do / Had he the motive and the cue for passion / That I have? (II. ii. 553–5); 'Who would fardels bear / To grunt and sweat under a weary life' (III. i. 76–7); 'Now could I drink hot blood / And do such bitter business as the day / Would quake to look on' (III. ii. 380–2); 'Now might I do it pat' (III. iv. 73); 'I do not know / Why yet I live to say "This thing's to do" ' (IV. iv. 43–4). In each of the seven soliloquies the idea is clear: Hamlet's life is one to be lived under the imposition of a great task, an imperious demand from outside. The speeches show him for a man taken up with the demands made upon him by that fact.

Of necessity, Hamlet pursues his course as revenger, scourge and minister, within a social group; but that group is not stable, it is itself disintegrating. Admittedly, the play barely invites its audience to see this as the disintegration of a whole society. It is less a political tragedy, and much more, in the wide sense, a domestic one, than *King Lear* or *Macbeth*. Nevertheless, the royal family with its entourage is there as a group: Hamlet is progressively alienated and isolated from it, and in its turn it is breaking into pieces. Ophelia loses her lover, her father, her reason and her life. Claudius is obliged to plan a second assassination; Hamlet brings about the death of his old school-fellows; Laertes plots revolt first, and murder to follow. As the play proceeds, it becomes clear that the audience is invited to widen its gaze beyond the protagonist himself, and to see his increasingly disastrous relation to his fellows as the central case of something happening everywhere.

These fairly obvious facts about the developing spectacle of the play have been given some surprising expression. 'To Hamlet comes the command of a great act—revenge . . . a sick soul is commanded to heal, to cleanse, to create harmony. But good cannot come of evil: it is seen that the sickness of his soul only further infects the state—his disintegration spreads out, disintegrating', writes Professor Knight; closely echoed by Mr

Traversi, who speaks of 'the disease which, emanating from Hamlet himself, expands from his wounded nature to cover the entire action'. [18] Were these references to spreading and expanding to mean only that at the beginning, Hamlet alone is in an unhappy condition, but that the others become so as the play goes on, little would have been said, and there would be little need to dissent from it. Professor Knight's reference to Hamlet's sick soul 'infecting' the state, however, suggests that Hamlet is to be seen not simply as the first to suffer from what later becomes general, but the cause of that change: in effect, that is, the source of the evil in the play. If something of this kind is meant (which is not wholly clear) one is entitled to see a certain whimsy in the idea that Shakespeare meant his play to depict the harm a society may incur from the disillusion of a man suffering from the familiar Jacobean disease of melancholy; and threw in regicide, usurpation and incest in the royal line to enliven the middle distance: for this is what would follow. But little harm is done by leaving an account of this sort as intact as it starts; so long as one bears in mind how amply the text puts forward another.

This other account is what follows from the most widespread of Elizabethan dramatic ideas in revenge tragedy: 'Blood will have blood.' 'Foul deeds will rise / Though all the earth o'erwhelm them to men's eyes', is almost Hamlet's first comment on hearing of the Ghost. He does not mean, of course, that the risen ghost itself is a foul deed, but that its apparition is the first sign of how some hidden wickedness, its nature yet unknown, is beginning to do what wickedness traditionally does, bring after itself a train of evil everywhere. The same implication is clear when the ghost is seen once more:

> *Hor:* Have after. *To what issue will this come?*
> *Mar:* Something is rotten in the state of Denmark,
> *Hor:* Heaven will direct it.
>
> (I. v. 89)

At the close of his first soliloquy, Hamlet has uttered the same inescapable idea:

> O, most wicked speed, to post
> With such dexterity to incestuous sheets!
> It is not, nor it *cannot, come to* good.
>
> (I. ii. 156)

Later, Rosenkranz and Guildenstern state the doctrine in all its
formality and solemnity. The passage expressed vital truths and
current dangers in Shakespeare's age, and it will sound banal
only to the brash and heedless modern ear:

> *Gil:* Most holy and religious fear it is
> To keep those many many bodies safe
> That live and feed upon your Majesty.
> *Ros:* The single and peculiar life is bound
> With all the strength and armour of the mind
> To keep itself from noyance; but much more
> That spirit upon whose weal depends and rests
> The lives of many. The cease of majesty
> Dies not alone, but like a gulf doth draw
> What's near it with it . . .
> . . . when it falls
> Each small annexment, petty consequence,
> Attends the boist'rous ruin. Never alone
> Did the king sigh, but with a general groan.
> (III. iii. 8)

The stinging irony of these words is plain. Claudius is not the
prop of social weal. He is the very man who knocked that prop
away, and by doing so initiated the movement of the play.
These lines tell us of exactly that progressive 'ruin' which we
must see it enact, as it goes forward, and of exactly what we
ought to recognize as the cause of that ruin. More clearly than
almost anywhere in this work, Shakespeare has made characters speak out of character (for it is scarcely to these two
pantaloons that one would turn for the principles of politics) in
order that their words may guide our eyes and minds as we
watch.

As for the actual quality of that progressive social ruin by
which Hamlet is surrounded, we may trace it symbolized, if we
wish, in the way that from Act III scene iv on to Act IV scene iv
the characters (and indeed men generally) are likened by the
imagery of the play more and more to beasts, without that
reason which makes men what they are. We may trace it in the
appearance of two other conventional ideas of the time, in
which rebellion transforms the ordered life of things on land into
the savage chaos of the sea, and the order of tradition into the
chaos of total new-fangledness:

Gent: The ocean, overpeering of his list,
Eats not the flats with more impitious haste
Than young Laertes, in a riotous head,
O'erbears your officers. The rabble call him lord;
And, as the world were but now to begin,
Antiquity forgot, custom unknown,
The ratifiers and props of every word,
They cry 'Choose we; Laertes shall be king'.
(IV. v. 96–103)

We may trace it yet again, if we wish, in how that most rigorous and solemn of duties in an early society, the fitting burial of the dead, begins to be no longer performed (Polonius, IV. v. 81; Ophelia, V. i. 229–32); a failure ironically pointing back not to the 'maimed rites' in the burial of Old Hamlet, but certainly to his sudden and chaotic death ('Unhousel'd, disappointed, unanel'd', iv. 77). We may see this in a sense ultimate sign of social chaos made general and symbolic in Hamlet's meditation (V. i) upon how the bodies of the dead, thrown up from their graves (this is the vital point), pass through every kind of wrong and senseless condition.

Finally, this whole movement in the action is symbolized in the spectacular tableau (it comes towards the close of Act V scene i), where the two young men of the play, soon to fight a duel using an unbaited and poisoned weapon, stand struggling in the open grave, surrounded by the rituals of death by suicide. But in thus tracing this movement through metaphor and symbol and fantasy and spectacle, we should remember that these things are not its primary vehicle; they help to make the movement pervasive and potent, but it is one which is embodied in the first instance in the action itself.

There are many plays in which, to put the matter baldly, the case of the *dramatis personae* gets worse as the play goes on. In *Hamlet* this occurs, in two ways, with a distinctive nuance. To begin with, over its whole length the play shows this degeneration into universal violence, conspiracy and chaos within the frame of a brilliant, exhilarating and yet (when once it is seen) disturbing and indeed fearful paradox. The world of *Hamlet*, as it declines into tragedy and chaos, yet maintains one part of itself always in a condition of exuberantly febrile life. Whatever else decays, there remains an incessant play and thrust of frenzied intrigue, of plot and counterplot, and on the surface of this, as its overt counterpart, a scintillating texture of intelligence and wit. Largely, this is the incomparable contribution of Hamlet himself; but not only so. Polonius plays his part at the beginning, Osric at the end. The grave-yard scene is almost an emblem of this paradox within the play: Hamlet's last and most extravagant ingenuities flash about that universal death, real on the stage and imagined by the actors, which is the state towards which the people of the play are heading all the time. This staggering hypertrophy of intelligence provides one large part of the delight and excitement; but another part, not exuberant, but none the less powerful for that, lies in our supervening awareness of how this play of wit iridesces upon the great *caput mortuum* which is coming into focus everywhere below it. Here is something surely unique in Shakespeare.

There is something else distinctive of the movement towards disaster in *Hamlet*. It is less sharply distinctive, because it is based upon a traditional conviction which both Shakespeare and others (notably Dante) have drawn upon. But this traditional conviction is worked out (as one could expect from the stress everywhere in this work upon fertile and witty ingenuity) with a complexity, thoroughness and repeated dexterity that have few parallels. The distinctive quality comes to light if the question is asked, *what kind* of event is it which carries the action (as we have seen, the progressive alienation of the dedicated protagonist from a society falling into chaos) stage by stage forward?

It might be the case that no answer could be given to that question; or the answer might be simply, various sorts of things occurring from time to time. But in the present case, the right answer seems somewhat more ambitious. There does seem to be a large design, which draws together most of the steps the play takes forward on its course, making them of one kind, and an illustration of one underlying idea; and we should be encouraged to trust what is suggested by attentive reading, when we notice that this is no distinctively modern pre-occupation. It is no idea coined by our contemporaries and read back into a work that comes from a past age, but one which (valid and massive as it is when recovered) is unfamiliar to us, although it lay at the centre of things in Shakespeare's own time.

A large proportion, perhaps most, of the main events which carry forward the action of this play, seem like chance events. They seem the work of 'Fortune' in her most casual, most random capacity. Polonius (II. ii. 111–17) misjudges the sincerity of Hamlet's love for Ophelia: it brings about her rejection of him, certainly has an important effect upon Hamlet himself, and plays its part in leading to Ophelia's madness and death. Yet of itself it seems not design, but pure unlucky accident. With it goes Polonius's other accidental error of judgement: that Ophelia's rejection is the cause of Hamlet's madness. This leads, along an improbable route, to the King's first sensing a real danger in Hamlet himself (III. i. 163). Rosenkranz and Guildenstern have arrived in Denmark at the 'hasty sending' of Claudius; but although they have not come by chance, it is the idea that they are the children of Fortune, of chance, which is strongly stressed at their first meeting with the Prince (II. ii. 230 ff). The players arrive (and one must bear in mind that their arrival is what makes possible the play scene and all that follows from it) entirely by chance (II. ii. 326). It is a chance that the one opportunity Hamlet had to kill Claudius proved no opportunity at all, because the King was praying; and another that this too was an error, because his praying was a sham. The killing of Polonius seems pure chance ('take thy Fortune', III. iv. 32); and so of course is Hamlet's meeting at sea with the pirates and subsequent return to Denmark.

All this side of the play seems to be epitomized and symbolized in the duel, greatest and most mortal of chances, at its end. Hamlet twice implies that he is himself the minion (darling or plaything) of Fortune. Speaking to Horatio, he mentions how men with one decisive defect, though they may be 'nature's livery or Fortune's star' (I. iv. 32), cannot but be discredited in the end. The speech has long been seen to apply ironically to Hamlet himself. Again, he later extols Horatio for being one of those

> Whose blood and judgement are so well comeddled
> That they are not a pipe for Fortune's finger
> To sound what stop she please

(III. ii. 64–7)

—which once more ironically implies that he, lacking Horatio's stoicism and calm resolve, is exactly such a plaything of Fortune himself. The idea is confirmed in a later scene, where he reproves Rosenkranz and Guildenstern for trying to 'sound' him as if he were a pipe, but only a moment later he says 'they fool me to the top of my bent', and thus realizes that here too, within limits, he is Fortune's mere victim. The final arrival of Fortinbras, which makes possible the close of the play in some sort of order, is again a pure chance.

Yet what *is* pure chance? The orthodox and traditional view still had a decisive strength in Pope's time, and permitted him to write 'All Chance, Direction which thou can'st not see'. This to Shakespeare was a central commonplace: perhaps its most eloquent and elaborate contemporary expression is the debate between Pamela and her wicked aunt in Sidney's *Arcadia*.[19] Here Sidney expends his ingenuity, as *avocatus diaboli*, in arguing that the seemingly random events of life are truly random; but the strong emotion and the eloquence appear in Pamela's reply, which argues that through all randomness runs ultimately, and decisively, the power and design of Providence. Randomness simply does not exist. All that exists is the operation, sometimes abrupt and direct, sometimes devious and slow, of Divine Justice.

Over and over in *Hamlet*, chance turns into a larger design, randomness becomes retribution. Polonius hides behind the arras so as to enable himself to explain everything: and he is silenced for ever ('thou find'st to be too busy is some danger', III. iv. 33). Rosenkranz and Guildenstern, bearing the sealed letters which order the death of Hamlet, go by just such letters, in altered form, to their deaths themselves. Hamlet, thinking how he will bring such a reversal about, says,

> Let it work
> For 'tis the sport to have the engineer
> Hoist with his own petar;
> (III. iv. 205-7)

—but the irony goes further than he sees: he has just afforded such sport himself. Killing Claudius (as he thought) at a time when he could do so scot-free, he has only, in killing Polonius, magnified all his difficulties. Claudius has been moving along just such a self-defeating path from the start, and says so:

> O limed soul, that struggling to be free
> Art more engaged . . .
> (III. iii. 68-9)

In the end, it is not from Hamlet's rapier that he dies ('O yet defend me friends; I am but hurt', V. ii. 316), but from the poisoned cup that he has himself prepared and that he has just tried to have passed to Hamlet: 'He is justly served / It is a poison tempered by himself', is Laertes' comment. As for the Queen, her death also comes, as retributively it should, in the intoxication and delight of the wine she has taken at the hand of Claudius. Laertes is the same. The rapier that he intends for Hamlet is that which kills him:

> *Osr:* How is't Laertes?
> *Laer:* Why, as a woodcock, to mine own springe, Osric;
> I am justly killed by mine own treachery
>
> (V. ii. 299)

All these things must be in Horatio's mind when, in the closing moments of the play, he says that he will give a public account of the whole bloodthirsty tangle, and culminates his summary of that account by speaking of

> purposes mistook
> Fall'n on the inventors' heads
> (V. ii. 376–7)

It is the same idea as that with which Dante closes Canto 28 of the *Inferno*: Bertrand de Born, in hell with his head severed forever because he severed father and son in rebellion, says, 'Cosi s'osserva in me lo contrapasso' (Thus retribution shows itself in me). Here, in this pervasive moving back upon itself of the work of Fortune, until it becomes the work of Destiny, transpires the radical organization and symmetry of the action; and in its repetition, its ingenious observance everywhere, something of what most distinguishes the play.

III

'OTHELLO'

FOR THE MODERN READER, *Othello* is perhaps the hardest of
all Shakespeare's tragedies to hold in perspective. Men's attitudes to the issues which appear in the play have greatly
changed between Shakespeare's time and our own; but in spite
of this, those issues are very far from having lost their interest.
They connect still with strong emotions, and emotions which are
easily provoked. Jealousy, fidelity, chastity, the quality of desire
between a man and a woman, the illicit or degenerate forms of
it, the rights which lovers have over each other, the proper
response to amorous treachery—these combine to make a subject of lively and indeed inflammable interest today. He who
writes of *Othello* cannot but write of them. On the other hand,
the spectacle of literary critics and university lecturers engaging
in disputes where to say anything worth saying, they must draw
upon their intimate comprehension of the many ways in which
sexuality may prove a good force or an evil one in men's lives, is
a spectacle which is not remote enough for comfort from the
ridiculous. All I can say is, that I hope the element of the ridiculous will be less prominent in this chapter than I have sometimes felt it to be in what (*Othello* aside) I have read so as to
write it.

The main purpose of the present chapter is to note and remove
certain factors which may make the reading of *Othello* abnormally
difficult for the modern reader; and when this is done, to notice
some main parts of what it offers for our experience, and to see
in what ways its action is taken beyond anything in *Hamlet*.

Othello issues from a society in which certain modes of thought, which to us have not simply lost their force, but become positively the expressions of the tyranny of the past, were perfectly familiar and acceptable. To recognize some of these shifts of attitude will help to read the play. One should have in mind that a critic's sensibility exercised upon a work will record certain findings; but findings both issue from, and breed, expectations. To an extent, we see what we want or expect to see, and having found one thing we begin to expect others. Historical knowledge of changes in outlook helps us to form these expectations, and also helps to control them. It may suggest to us to look for what we might otherwise have let escape us; and conversely, to be on our guard against finding something that we might confidently expect to find, if we lacked it. That something, to be sure, may still be there. Great writers sometimes leap beyond the consciousness of their time. But before we conclude that Shakespeare leapt beyond his time, and also landed in ours, we shall do well to look twice at his work, bringing into play what historical knowledge we have, and exercising a little distrust of ourselves. Distrust may be well placed. The impeccable and infallible critical sensibility could no doubt dispense with this as with all other aids; but I cannot think of anyone for whom this theoretical truth has practical utility.

Some readers may find that once Othello has come to believe that his wife is the mistress of his first officer, he is filled with venomous anger of what is really an irrelevant kind. He is not, they may say, filled simply with grief that a genuine bond of love had gone to pieces, or that what seemed like a fine person was really a despicable one; nor, perhaps, with embarrassment and shame that he could have made so abject a mistake about Desdemona himself. Some of these emotions may be traceable in him; but if so, they combine with another which is far less to his credit. This is an indignant sense of personal affront, of an outrage to his dignity and his personal rights, almost something like his property rights.

> I will chop her into messes. Cuckold me!
> (IV. i. 196)

It is not, to be sure, the dominant reaction in Othello, but it is noticeably there; and the modern reader, in his turn, can con-

ceivably take it as an affront to his sense of the equality of men
and women in matters of love.

If the modern reader goes on, however, to take this as part of
what the play points to as defective in Othello, he runs into
danger. Such findings need very full support, because they
would run counter to what would have seemed perfectly normal in Shakespeare's own time. Othello's affronted indignation
should be seen against the background of the Elizabethan
prayer-book, where in the marriage service the husband promises to cherish and comfort his wife, but the wife to serve and
obey the husband. It should be seen against this passage from
Latimer's First Sermon before King Edward VI (1549):

Christ limiteth us to one wife only; and it is a great thing for a man
to rule one wife rightly and ordinately. For a woman is frail, and
proclive unto all evils; a woman is a very weak vessel, and may soon
deceive a man and bring him unto all evils. Many examples have we
in holy scripture. [Latimer instances Eve and Jezebel.] It is a very
hard thing for a man to rule one woman well.

The reference in this passage to a woman's deceiving her husband is not to her being unfaithful, but to her actually leading
him into sin; the two main points, however, that all women are
naturally more inclined towards sinfulness than men, and that a
woman should (in recognition, indeed, of this) be subject to her
husband, are very relevant to the play. All this is in harmony
with, say, so traditional a source of guidance on the subject as
Numbers 30, where it is laid down that a woman's promises
and undertakings may be overridden by her father while she is
not married, and by her husband when she is. The only caveat is
that the man must disown her undertaking at once, if he is to do
so at all: this being a safeguard for others, not for her.

At least once, Shakespeare wholeheartedly endorses this
standpoint. He does so in *The Taming of the Shrew*, where
Katharine's closing speech must be taken as without a hint of
irony, and as expressing the correct and traditional doctrine
proper for the case. (I have seen it proposed that this speech
should be acted ironically: to do so would simply be a vulgar
modern trick.) In fact, shortly before Katharine quotes the
reference in the marriage rite to how women in marriage are
'bound to serve, love and obey', she outlines the Elizabethan

sense of the relation between man and wife, and does something
to elucidate it to a modern reader.

> Thy husband is thy lord, thy life, thy keeper,
> Thy head, thy sovereign; one that cares for thee,
> And for thy maintenance commits his body
> To painful labour both by sea and land,
> To watch the night in storms, the day in cold,
> Whilst thou liest warm at home, secure and safe
> And craves no other tribute at thy hands
> But love, fair looks, and true obedience—
> Too little payment for so great a debt.
> Such duty as the subject owes the prince,
> Even such a woman oweth to her husband.
>
> (V. ii. 146)

Othello's sense that in being unfaithful (as he thinks) Desdemona
has not merely destroyed an equal and joint possession, but done
a personal wrong to him, must be seen in the kind of context
which these passages suggest. Shakespeare indeed might have
been reaching forward to a new attitude, and wishing his
audience to see something defective in his response; but we
shall do well at least to try out carefully whether Shakespeare
saw this matter as his age did; just as we shall do well, if we jib
at Othello's believing at all that his own wife could be unfaithful, to remember the passage about a woman's being proclive
unto all evil; or if we think it somehow a mark of folly or defect
to be inclined to trust a male friend (the long-valued Iago)
before his wife, to remember the strong conviction of the period
that this would be the natural choice dictated by the wisdom
(in the best sense) of tradition, and the over-riding claims of
friendship.

   Othello is also, some have felt, unduly conscious of his great
public position. This is linked with his indignation against
Desdemona:

> *Iago:* O, 'tis foul in her.
> *Oth:* With mine officer!
> *Iago:* That's fouler.
>
> (IV. i. 197)

The modern reader will feel that this response is not easily seen
as to do with true love. But again, there is a distinction to be

born in mind between Shakespeare's time and our own. Today, we admire great men who can seem all the time to forget their greatness, who strike the note of the ordinary and human, and are all informality. 'Condescension' is a term of unmitigated abuse. To the Elizabethans, and long after indeed, this would have seemed wrong-headed and strange. To them, a man in great place should never forget his great place: he should never act like an ordinary man.[20] If we remember that Othello was a prince by his birth, and only one below a prince by his office, the following account in the most famous of sixteenth-century conduct manuals on how a prince should behave will prove to the point:

> . . . hee ought to accompany with his greatness a familiar gentle be-
> haviour, with a soft and lovely kindness . . . and good cast to make
> much of his subjects and straungers, discreetly more and lesse, accord-
> ing to their deserts, observing alwaies notwithstanding the majesty
> meet for his degree . . .[21]

Shakespeare was steadily making Othello conform to this kind of requirement. Time and again, his conduct is impeccably correct in just this way.

> Good signior, you shall more command with years
> Than with your weapons . . .
>
> (I. ii. 160)

he says to Brabantio, with exactly the justified hint of deferential reproof. The poise is maintained when Brabantio demands that he go to prison to await trial by law:

> What if I do obey?
> How may the Duke be therewith satisfied,
> Whose messengers are here about my side,
> Upon some present business of the state . . .
>
> (I. ii. 87)

To the Venetian Senate he begins:

> Most potent, grave and reverend signiors,
> My very noble and approved good masters.
>
> (I. iii. 76)

In the dismissal of Cassio, though the moment is a peculiarly provoking one, and Othello has said that he is beginning to be riled, Shakespeare still makes him say neither more nor less than the just man must: 'Cassio, I love thee, / But never more be officer of mine' (II. iii. 240), and he continues with the same measured solicitude for the claims of one and all, Desdemona in the first place:

> . . . See if my gentle love be not roused up.
> I'll make thee an example.
> *Des:* What is the matter, dear?
> *Oth:*   All's well now sweeting;
> Come away to bed. (*To Montano*) Sir, for your hurts,
> Myself will be your surgeon. Lead him off.
> Iago, look with care about the town,
> And silence those whom this vile brawl distracted.

All the time, Othello is accompanying his greatness with a soft and lovely kindness, and good cast to make much of his subjects, discreetly more and less, observing always notwithstanding the majesty meet for his own degree. Short of explaining in a Preface, like Dryden, Shakespeare could not have made clearer his intention to portray the great and good man in the then accepted sense. The contrast with Antony ill-using a messenger, Coriolanus constantly losing his head and being reproved by his supporters, Lear calling his first councillor a recreant, could not be clearer.

At this point, it may be asked whether the same degree of integrity, propriety and distinction can be claimed for Othello's attitudes and conduct in his domestic life, as I have been claiming for his public; and it is well known, no doubt, that this has been denied in lively terms. The Appendix to this chapter will examine the strength of one such denial; here it is to the point to notice how much Othello is made to say (prior, of course, to his becoming jealous) which makes him clearly seem a model not only of affection, but also of trust, consideration, and generosity towards Desdemona. He offers to leave the rebutting of Brabantio's charges to her testimony alone. When he joins in asking leave for her to go with him to Rhodes, he utters a speech which there is no ground whatever to take as insincere and scheming, and which could not make clearer what we are to see, and what we are not, in his request:

Desd:	Let me go with him.
Oth:	Let her have your voice.

Vouch with me, heaven, I therefore beg it not
To please the palate of my appetite;
Nor to comply with heat—the young affects
In me defunct—and proper satisfaction;
But to be free and bounteous to her mind.

(I. iii. 259)

Othello continues, in another sense, to be bounteous to Desdemona's mind even after he has become convinced of her being a strumpet. His passion of vindictive fury has still to struggle against the delight he had taken in everything which made her a complete person:

Oth: Hang her! I do but say what she is: so delicate with her needle, an admirable musician—O, she will sing the savageness out of a bear!—of so high and plenteous wit and invention.

Iago: She's the worse for all this.

Oth: O, a thousand, a thousand times—and then to be of so gentle a condition.

Iago: Ay, too gentle.

(IV. i. 182)

Earlier on, too, Othello expresses sentiments which (much more clearly in Shakespeare's time than in ours) show him as a model among husbands:

'Tis not to make me jealous
To say my wife is fair, feeds well, loves company,
Is free of speech, sings, plays and dances well;
Where virtue is, these are more virtuous.

(III. iii. 187)

Finally, to come to in a sense more intimate matters, his invitation to Desdemona on the wedding night is again a model of gentleness, courtesy and sense of mutuality:

Come, my dear love,
The purchase made, the fruits are to ensue;
That profit's yet to come 'twixt me and you.

(II. iii. 8)

Just before this, he has asked Cassio to look to the guard that night, and not indulge overmuch in festivities:

> Let's teach ourselves that honorable stop,
> Not to outsport discretion.

By the obvious relevance of this to Othello's own situation at the time, Shakespeare takes one more opportunity of presenting him as the 'Complete Man'.

Some readers of this play have been struck, however, by Othello's consciousness of Desdemona physically, or more particularly by his capacity to contemplate her physically in contradistinction to her as a person. Perhaps Othello says nothing which carries such sensuous bluntness, and so clearly sees in the office of the body a separate and distinguishable thing, as a phrase which the husband (but not the wife) uttered in the Elizabethan marriage service: 'with my body I thee worship'. This aside, however, once Othello has become convinced that Desdemona is morally evil, there are only two things that he can possibly do. One would be to cease to think her beautiful, or at least cease to find her attractive. A few readers, perhaps, will find this natural or at least hanker after it; to most it will at once seem absurd. When Othello takes the only alternative course, and dwells with horrified astonishment upon the paradox of Desdemona's external loveliness and (as he supposes) internal deformity, we should call to mind once again that some ideas familiar for Shakespeare have dropped out of men's consciousness by now.

For ourselves, the very idea that men or women may be beautiful—as opposed to attractive, distinguished-looking, or a variety of other terms of narrow significance—has become unfashionable and even slightly embarrassing; and the idea that beautiful people may be (in the most general sense) more virtuous than others has dropped out of currency—(though there may be much in it: virtue being easier for those to whom life is often easier). In Shakespeare's time the idea was widely accepted and also widely challenged. It was a topical issue which aroused interest.

> So every spirit, as it is most pure,
> And hath in it the more of heavenly light,
> So it the fairer body doth procure
> To habit in . . .
> For of the soule the bodie forme doth take . . .

44

This is what Spenser wrote in the *Hymn to Beauty*. Ovid and Horace, on the other hand, said that good looks with modesty were rare. Both views—naturally—are quoted in Burton's *Anatomy of Melancholy*.[22] Bacon gives the whole first half of his essay *Of Beauty* to discussing how beauty and virtue may be related. The issue was as live then as it is dead now. That it was live for Othello is clear; and it is this, rather than anything less to his credit, that we should see in one or two of this speeches.

Burton also helps a little, perhaps, in the matter of Othello's jealousy. Frankly, this is a subject on which some critics have written what ought to make one distrust one's eyes. When Mr Traversi (inveigled for a moment into a Bradleyan speculation which is not the kind of criticism he takes his stand by) writes '(Iago) must have been very sure of the Moor's blindness to work upon him with so gross a caricature',[23] it is perhaps enough to recall what working upon someone with a gross caricature looks like in a play. This happens, for example, in the conversation between Malcolm and Macduff (*Macbeth*, IV. iv). Malcolm attributes a string of grandiose vices to himself, and Macduff apparently believes him, although he already knows him well. If this is not enough, perhaps one should compare Iago's deception of Othello with, say, that of Gloucester by Edmund, or Timon by his flatterers. By this time, it will be clear that Iago's tissue of hints and withdrawals, of particularities dissolving into generalities, of soothing and provocation, is clearly the least gross and least a caricature of all Shakespeare's efforts in this direction; and if, even so, a gross caricature is what it still looks like, we shall feel inclined to wonder whether Shakespeare was preoccupied exclusively with characters imposing on each other by gross caricatures, or ever, instead, portrayed one imposing on another by subtle distortion and Machiavellian skill: whether he ever attempted this and what it would look like if he did.

When Dr Leavis, in a moment of uncharacteristic rashness, writes 'Othello has from the beginning responded to Iago . . . with a promptness that couldn't be improved on',[24] light may again be thrown on the matter by recalling other plays. If we do this, we shall at once find reason to think that Othello's promptness could very much have been improved upon; and it will not be his promptness but his slowness which will impress. Angelo in *Measure for Measure*, for example, is by comparison with Othello a responder of electric swiftness. The earliest point at which one can suppose that Angelo is beginning actually to succumb to Isabella's sexual attraction is in Act II scene ii l. 133, where in response to her implying that one in authority might sin like him over whom he has authority, he perfunctorily asks 'Why do you put these sayings upon me?' (it is a most beautiful instance of how Shakespeare could depict the embarrassment of incipient emotion). Thirty lines later, his overmastering desire to possess Isabella physically is fully formed: he makes that clear in l. 171 ('Shall we desire to raze the sanctuary . . .?'). Whether even Shakespeare could have improved upon this celerity may, if we wish, be doubted.

How prompt is Othello? Iago makes the first move in Act III scene iii l. 94. Seventy-seven lines later, by using the word 'cuckold', Iago brings into view for the first time what he is going to say; but he uses that word in so general, brief and cryptic a context, that Othello still seems not quite to see what is going to be brought up. After another thirty lines, Iago gets at last so far as to say

> Look to your wife; observe her well with Cassio

—though he adds that he does not advise Othello to be jealous. Othello himself takes the first step towards jealousy itself after another thirty lines: but it is an extremely small step. After a series of brief answers which show how his mind is busy in silence, and immediately after saying 'I do not think but Desdemona's honest', he adds, still it seems with the voice of thought speaking aloud but half unconscious of any external audience:

> And yet how nature erring from herself—

and at that he breaks off. He has seen that it is not in principle impossible for Desdemona to deceive him. An explanation for such a deed could be found. It is indeed in woman's nature to do what is against nature. He has remembered (and this, by the way, is a repeated impression with Othello, and an instance of Shakespeare's insight into the depiction of character) the book, or remembered something he has been told. The case lies outside his experience, almost outside his credence; but he seems to be remembering something he has learnt maxim-fashion, and to realize that it would afford an explanation of what, left to himself, he would find bewildering.

These details, by themselves, count for much. They count for more, if we recall that the question is not of life itself, but of a play. Shakespeare expends almost one twentieth of the length of the whole work in bringing the protagonist merely to a point where he sees that Desdemona's infidelity is not in principle out of the question. Beside what other play is this 'promptness that couldn't be improved on'?

We thus demonstrate (that is the word), not that Othello becomes jealous with unbelievable slowness or not at all, but simply the plain pedestrian fact which stares a reader or an audience in the face; that when Othello later says he was one 'not easily jealous', he is not offering the audience inconvenience and confusion. As is so common in Shakespeare, and so clear a sign of his mastery of the theatre, he is offering us help and guidance. Shakespeare is using his character as mouthpiece, and telling us how to watch his play. We need not imitate Morgan writing on Falstaff, and prefer our own ingenuity to his.

Before his jealousy begins, then, Othello is outstanding, he is the Renaissance Complete Man in both his public and his private life. If this is not seen, what happens to him once jealousy begins to take possession of him is not seen, and the play is not seen. That so plain a finding should need to be argued at length is reason for surprise; yet certainly, at the present time, the need exists. What, however, finally confirms this view of Othello, is the unanimous testimony about him which is given by the other characters. If he had always been inwardly a failure as a man, and been driven mainly by self-regard and voluptuous sensuality, they are one and all hopelessly in error about him. In this case Shakespeare's play, as it progresses, would impose more and more forcefully upon its audience a question which it does absolutely nothing to begin to answer: what special talent has Othello, and what special weakness has his society, that none of those who surround him, not even his wife, not even her experienced and cynical waiting-woman, should ever glimpse his defects—those, that is, which he is alleged to have had all the time—but on the contrary should unite to praise him?

47

Othello is not praised simply for his talents as a mercenary
general, or his courage, or his powers of command. He is praised,
over and over, for his more intimate qualities of mind and
character; and what the others say of him is the more convincing, because it chimes in so well with what they ought by convention to say of one whom the author is seeing as the 'Complete
Man' within the perspective of his own age. Lodovico, towards
the end, records what the Venetian Senate had thought of
Othello at the beginning, and endorses it as he does so:

> Is this the noble Moor, whom our full senate
> Call all in all sufficient? Is this the nature
> Whom passion could not pierce?
>
> (IV. i. 261)

(The last words should remind us once again of how deeply
Shakespeare's play is set within the moral world of its time.)
Indirectly, this opinion of Othello receives support from Emilia,
when she tells Cassio, after the brawl, what Othello has said
about him:

> The General and his wife are talking of it;
> And she speaks for you stoutly: The Moor replies
> That he you hurt is of great fame in Cyprus
> And great affinity, and that in wholesome wisdom
> He might not but refuse you; but he protests he loves you
> And needs no other suitor but his likings
> To take the safest occasion by the front
> To bring you in again.
>
> (III. i. 43–50)

For Emilia to quote her master in this straightforward and
sympathetic way, is for her to leave the audience with the impression that so far as she is concerned, when Othello speaks of
'wholesome wisdom' he knows his subject. Elsewhere Iago goes
out of his way to express grudging praise, carrying all the more
weight for that, of an enemy:

> The Moor (howbeit I endure him not)
> Is of a constant, loving, noble nature,
> And I dare think, he'll prove to Desdemona
> A most rare husband.
>
> (II. i. 282)

Finally, Desdemona herself—and it is after her wedding night, which was a real one ('look if my gentle love be not roused up') —has no doubts about Othello's nature:

> *Des:* Where should I lose the handkerchief, Emilia?
> *Emil:* I know not, madam.
> *Des:* Believe me, I had rather lose my purse
> Full of crusadoes; and but my noble Moor
> Is true of mind, and made of no such baseness
> As jealous creatures are, it were enough
> To put him to ill thinking.
>
> (III. iv. 20–8)

These lines do more than add Desdemona's testimony to those of the others. If Othello was really imposed upon by a gross caricature, her anxiety here is a disquieting error of judgement; and those who have seen so much ill in Othello's nature might begin to look for signs of an over-suspicious nature, prone to sympathize with self-dramatizing blindness, or even voluptuous sensuality, in her. Perhaps, like Mr Traversi, they can bring themselves to convict Cassio of seeing Desdemona as 'a choice morsel to be contemplated, tasted, and enjoyed'[25] merely because (avoiding an argument) he stands aloof from Iago's prurient remarks about her by carefully chosen phrases like 'She is a most exquisite lady', 'Indeed, she is a most fresh and delicate creature', 'An inviting eye; and yet methinks right modest'. In that case, they will have no difficulty with Desdemona. Her finding suspicion natural will damn her, just as easily as the suspicion itself damns Othello; but this important clue to the play's meaning has been overlooked by those who could most exploit it. *

Desdemona's remark, quoted above, about the sun having drawn jealous humours from Othello, means more to the audience than it does to her. Burton's *Anatomy* makes it clear that the sun operated quite otherwise: the hot climate makes southern men (especially, he adds in an aside in which he might even have had Othello in mind, those who live near Carthage)

---

* The diligent reader will recall that Desdemona may be an exhibitionist (IV. ii. 106), incipient sadist (III. iii. 24–5), conspicuous masochist showing infantile regression (IV. ii. 113–14), necro-philiac (IV. iii. 23–4), incipiently very promiscuous (IV. i. 227, IV. ii. 108, IV. iii. 34), and also, quite possibly, a frequenter of public houses (II. i. 138).

capable of very extreme jealousy.[26] This is the counterpart of the belief, so gratifying even today to the whole of one half of Europe and a few of the other half, that southern nations are more passionate than northern ones. Othello is past his youth, and several passages (some have been quoted) make it clear that he is not to be seen as an abnormally passionate man; but the other part of the formula covers him. He is 'not easily jealous', but once he becomes jealous at all he is jealous very intensely; and our awareness of this process is a large part of our experience throughout the play.

There is, in this play, less sense than in *Hamlet*, and indeed there is virtually no sense at all, of a society which is swept along with the protagonist and suffers a decline parallel to his own. Othello undergoes the dynamic of the play virtually by himself, and indeed it is part of the nature of the central change that it should be an inner and almost a solitary one. What is that change? Nothing short of this, that the complete man becomes a complete monster:

> I see, sir, you are eaten up with passion
> (III. iii. 395)

Reason abdicates as sovereign in Othello, and his rational nature as a man is destroyed. The idea of the monster is reiterated:

> *Oth:*   By heaven, he echoes me
> As if there were some monster in his thought
> Too hideous to be shown.
> (III. iii. 110–12)

'A monster / Begot upon itself, born on itself,' says Emilia of jealousy later (III. iv. 162). At the end, Montano's first words when he is confronted by the outcome of Othello's jealousy are 'O monstrous act!' (V. ii. 193). The monster is made real in one particular image which adds a significant further idea.

> I had rather be a toad
> And live upon the vapour of a dungeon,
> Than keep a corner in the thing I love
> For other's uses.
> (III. iii. 274–6)

Here the monster becomes embodied (the idea is echoed in

Othello's later horrified thought of the 'cistern for foul toads / To knot and gender in', IV. ii. 62) in the supposedly poisonous creature ('The Moor already changes with my poison', says Iago, III. iii. 329) that lives alone, and on nothing.

Othello's progressive isolation throughout the play is quite as clearly marked as that of Hamlet, and in some ways the total shape of this change, and its essential nature, are a great deal more so. There is no further need to stress how, when the play opens, Othello is a man esteemed, admired and valued on every hand. His position of privilege is greater than that of Hamlet; he appears at the centre not only of the ceremonial but also of the active life of the state: its most solicited man and its leader in war. Nor does his progressively losing this position until he is isolated from all others need proof in detail. Apart from Iago and Brabantio, it is Cassio from whom he is first cut off. The leave-taking, begun by Othello, is a formal one:

> Cassio, I love thee;
> But never more be officer of mine.
> (II. iii. 240)

In Act III scene iii, Emilia deserts Othello's cause, though in ignorance, when she says that she will give up the handkerchief to Iago; and what is happening to the protagonist is underlined by the leave-taking, enacted twice over, and rendered prominent and even solemn, between Iago and himself (III. iii. 244–62). On this being completed, Othello is left conspicuously on the stage alone. When, in front of Lodovico newly from Venice, he persistently orders Desdemona to leave him ('Get you away! . . . Hence, avaunt!') the process of isolation (once more underlined, made almost a ceremony, by Desdemona's going, returning and going again) is carried a stage further, at the very time when the protagonist's essential link with his whole society is being loosened. We hear, that is to say, that he is relieved of his command in Cyprus (Cassio takes his place), and must return to Venice. There is no question of his returning in disfavour, but that he is returning in triumph is very much not suggested; and whether or not he is going to remote Mauretania, as Iago adds, he is now very strangely in the position of a man who has lost his bonds with others, whose status in his society has been suspended, or is even dissolving.

Again, moreover, the protagonist invites the audience to watch him in a distinctive way, as a man who commits himself to a recognizable rôle. At the end of Act III scene iii, Othello dedicates himself to the rôle of revenger in a formalized, ritualized scene much like that in *Hamlet*:

> Look here, Iago—
> All my fond love thus do I blow to heaven.
> 'Tis gone.
> Arise black vengeance from the pit of Hell.
> (III. iii. 448)

A piece of stage business, invented for the occasion, underlines the moment in one way; while the invocation of the powers of evil does so in another. When Iago, a moment later, kneels and swears in his turn, the irony of the occasion is enriched, in that the good man has invoked hell, and the evil one heaven ('Witness, you ever-burning lights above'); but the fact itself, that at this crucial moment of self-committal to his rôle Othello should invoke the evil powers, is something which has parallels in the later plays. Moreover, it is now that Othello delivers one of the most famous of all his speeches, that in which he says that his 'Bloody thoughts' shall sweep onward like the sea; we have the traditional comparison, at this most significant of all moments, with what for Shakespeare's contemporaries was the supreme instance of violent chaos, of a Nature whose nature was above all others to err from itself: the sea, a world of total and ferocious chaos. To an attentive and informed audience, Shakespeare has displayed not only what happened, but precisely what we ought to think of it; the whole quality of the occasion, irrevocable and disastrous, stands clearly revealed.

Later, when Othello laments that Heaven has made him

> The fixed figure for the time of scorn
> To point his slow and moving finger at
> (IV. ii. 55–6)

he is not drawing attention merely to the fact that an integral part of his supposed misfortune is to be silently ridiculed as a cuckold; implicitly, he is also reinforcing the general impression of himself as someone singled out by the play to pursue a distinctive course and to be watched and observed as he pursues it. Another aspect of this is his speaking of himself in the third person: 'Where shall Othello go?', and 'that's he that was Othello. Here I am' (V. ii. 274; V. ii. 287). We ought no more to see in this a kind of self-dramatizing which merits condemnation, than we should in Lear's 'O Lear, Lear, Lear' or 'The king would speak with Cornwall', or 'It is I, Hamlet the Dane', or 'I am Antony yet'. These are simply not invitations to busy ourselves with character. They invite us to register, with unusual distinctiveness and conclusiveness, the situation of a protagonist who is undergoing, or has undergone, a distinctive experience. Even the character himself is beginning to see his case as such, so much is he a man marked out from others: the invitation to the audience to do the same is all the stronger.

So it is with Othello. The invitation is extended to us once again, with the same distancing impersonality, in the words of Lodovico almost at the end, when the time has come for a summing-up of the whole event of the drama. Ludovico speaks of Othello in a way which confirms (if confirmation were still needed) much of the plain-dealing account of the play advanced in this chapter:

> O thou Othello, that was once so good,
> *Fall'n* in the practice of a damned slave
> What shall be said of thee?
> (V. ii. 294–6)

A great event has occurred, filling the whole volume of the play; and towards the end of it both the *dramatis personae* and we ourselves have to seize its wholeness and come to understand it.

What Othello advances himself (there is barely a parallel to this anywhere in *Hamlet*) is the idea that through the course of the play he has travelled as if on a journey, and the closing scene has brought him to a point at which there is no going further:

> Here is my journey's end, here is my butt,
> And very sea-mark of my utmost sail.
> (V. ii. 270–1)

Othello is speaking, most immediately, of the weapon he has found in the chamber ('it was a sword of Spain, the ice-brook's temper'); but this edge to what he says does not strike at once. It is a private irony, savoured as yet only by himself. In the main, the 'journey's end', the sea-mark of Othello's utmost sail, is the situation in which he now is; and the journey is not life at large, in a vague sense, but the journey of a protagonist, the journey of a play.

The sharpest difference between the experience of Hamlet, and that of Othello, is not that Othello's experience has a more clearly marked end: but that it is more clearly articulated throughout. Hamlet may show effects of stress, but Othello's whole nature is transformed, and transformed in a coherent sequence. He becomes a man possessed; and this unseats his rational nature until he is entirely blind to truth, and disrupts his emotional nature until the emotions which he once gave least rein to, now entirely possess him. At almost the end, when he is in effect driven mad ('alas, why gnaw you so your nether lip?'), he destroys the centre of his own life, and emerges as a nature which has been wholly ruined. It is perhaps going too far to say that he consciously tries to deceive Emilia over her mistress's death: the moment is too intricate and charged to bear this account. His feeble, evasive, shambling answers are simply, for a moment, those of a broken man. As he says himself:

> I am not valiant neither—
> But every puny whipster gets my sword.
> (V. ii. 246–7)

Yet this collapse is not all.

Othello pulls himself together. The response which disaster evokes in him is symbolized plainly for the audience in the loss of one sword and the finding of the other; and this second sword, no chance find, but the tried strength of Othello at his best. His response is twofold; a recovery of the reason which enables him to comprehend, exactly and almost at once, the full nature of what he has done:

> Will you, I pray, demand that demi-devil
> Why he hath thus ensnar'd my *soul* and *body*?
> (V. ii. 304–5)

and more striking than this, a recovery of the will, after its moment of prostration, which enables him at the end not simply to commit suicide and to win space and attention (or rather, inattention) enough to do so, but genuinely to dominate the stage in terms of moral fibre; to be the great man once again, to whom it falls (as it does not to Hamlet, Lear, Macbeth, any other of Shakespeare's tragic heroes) to render the final account of his career while the other actors, and the audience, merely listen.

This view is not (to speak with restraint) universally acclaimed; and Othello's speech immediately before he stabs himself has been the object of some disparaging comment. Mr Eliot has said that Othello is 'cheering himself up'. Dr Leavis has used the words 'self-dramatization' and 'un-self-comprehending', has alleged that the tears Othello sheds are for the pathos of 'the spectacle of himself' (not, as one might suppose, for the major facts of the case), and suggests finally that in the closing lines Othello recalls, and re-enacts, 'his supreme moment of deliberate courage'. This—another attempt, be it noted, to don the tattered plumes of Bradley, and wing with them back before the play opens, or to and fro over a character's whole career— will not do. To have intervened in a street brawl, and (though in an unfriendly town) stabbed a man who may not even have been a soldier, is so far from looking like the supreme moment of deliberate courage in the life of a successful mercenary general, that on its own merits it is self-evidently a minor incident in that life.

That is a detail, though. What is not a detail is that it seems as if both these critics, when they wrote what they did of the speech, were unaware of the convention within which it is written, and therefore of what must be looked for in it and how it must be judged. The last spech of a hero is no piece of private musing, but a conventional *genre*. It is the moment at which the character has a special privilege of comment: to sum up either his own life and what it stood for, or the causes of his death. These conventions are widespread in Elizabethan drama, but the cases of Gaunt, Hotspur, King Henry IV, Warwick in Henry VI, Hamlet and Antony make the point clear. All these either speak in the convention, or begin to but are prevented by death itself. It is also Othello's convention. His words should fall with an impersonality, and formality, upon the listener's ear. They are an authoritative and exact account of what has happened in the play. The character is stepping forward from his

part to speak with the voice of that implicit chorus which so
often speaks in Shakespeare.

What, then, of the seemingly irrelevant anecdote of the
closing lines?

> Set you down this:
> And say besides that in Aleppo once,
> Where a malignant and a turban'd Turk
> Beat a Venetian and traduc'd the state,
> I took by th' throat the circumcised dog,
> And smote him—thus.
>
> (V. ii. 355–9)

It is not irrelevance. It is no mere self-indulgent re-enactment
of a supreme or any other moment in Othello's past. Othello
has been led to it by what he said two sentences before: that he
is

> one whose hand
> *Like the base Indian*, threw away a pearl
> Richer than all his tribe
>
> (V. ii. 349–51)

He sees that he has not lived like a Venetian, but like a savage;
and the idea leads him to the anecdote which, by its intense
ironic charge, offers the final comment upon what he has done,
offers a decisive comprehension of it. He has seen that the Turk,
chief enemy of Venice, and the Moor, have become one. The
'circumcised dog' is himself. For what has Othello done in the
case of Desdemona, daughter of a Senator, but 'beat a Venetian
and traduce the state'? The earlier incident swims ironically up
from the past because it reveals the ultimate contour of the
present; and there is one sense in which Othello does indeed re-
enact his past deed: he took vengeance on a little enemy of his
society then, and this makes it clearer that he is doing the same
thing upon a great one, now. The justice he wrought upon
Desdemona was a false justice. This is not. The pattern of the
tragedy is complete at last.

IV

'MACBETH'

THERE IS a clear sense, in *Hamlet* and to a lesser extent in *Othello*, that a retributive justice works through human life, and that an order and symmetry may therefore be seen in the doings of men. In *Macbeth* this is more conspicuous still. First, it is a substantial part of the whole movement of the action. Moreover, the action itself is seen in a perspective which extends beyond the doings of men, since it takes in the environment of Nature within which these doings occur, and from which in the end they seem to derive their quality. *Macbeth*, that is to say, is a work which offers the spectator no view of life alone, but a view of life which is part of a view of the world. In a broad and perhaps old-fashioned sense of the term, it is a philosophical play as *Hamlet* and *Othello* are not.

What opens up this wider perspective of life is nothing short of the play's total dynamic; but this includes far more than any mere 'what happens to the characters' seen in simple terms. The characters, taken in themselves, have to thread their way through an ampler body of experience proffered to the spectator; and for him, this ampler body of experience, this poetic richness of the play, is less conspicuous as chains of imagery which he could list as mere words in his study, than as images in the true sense, images which seem to people the stage, which have an independent life in the experience before him. It is in this sense, a sense which takes us beyond 'language' considered by itself, that *Macbeth* is a more than realistic, a truly poetic play.

At the opening of *Macbeth*, Macbeth himself is the centre of respect and interest. He is the cynosure, the present saviour of the state.

> . . . brave Macbeth—well he deserves that name—
> Disdaining Fortune, with his brandish'd steel
> Which smoked with bloody execution,
> Like *valour's minion*, carv'd out his passage . . .
>
> (I. ii. 16)

With these vivid words, the absent is present: the minion of valour and disdainer of Fortune is sharply before our imagination in all the slaughter of civil war. Yet this image of Macbeth is ambivalent. Only a few lines before, in the explosive opening words of the very first scene (other than that of the witches, no clear part of human life at all), Shakespeare has provided his audience, before their eyes and on stage, with an actual picture that the account of Macbeth in battle, quoted just now, disquietingly resembles:

> What bloody man is that? He can report,
> As seemeth by his plight, of the *revolt*
> The newest state.
>
> (I. ii. 1)

But insofar as we identify Macbeth with the image of a man stained in blood, and his weapon dripping with blood, he is no image merely of a destroyer of revolt. By a more direct and primitive mode of thought, by simple association, he is an image of revolt itself. The doubtful goodness of his disdaining Fortune (of which more must be said later) appears in a new, uneasy light.

This image of the bloody man is so much insisted on in the opening scenes, that it is not enough to call it an image. It is an apparition. It haunts the stage. Ross says that Macbeth was:

> Not afraid of what thyself didst make,
> Strange *images of death*.
>
> (I. iii. 96)

Again, the ambiguous phrasing carries weight. It is the same hideous sight which is the 'horrid image' seen by Macbeth, in imagination, after his meeting with the witches (I. iii. 135); and that we see, in Macbeth himself, when he enters after the murder of Duncan, and invites our contemplation almost as if he were an emblem of violence ('this is a sorry sight', II. ii. 20). Again, it is the same image that we must call to mind when Macbeth says that he will not return to see the spectacle of the murdered Duncan (II. ii. 50); and that Lady Macbeth says she will make the grooms look like; and that Lennox revives once more for us in his account of the grooms ('their hands and faces were all badged with blood' (II. iii. 100). It is 'the great doom's image' that Macbeth himself sees in Duncan lying dead when he tells the lords of the murder (II. iii. 60). This image, kept so much before our imagination that it seems without exaggeration to stalk the stage, is the image with which Macbeth is identified in the very first account we have of him. From the start, he may be valour's minion, but he impresses our minds as the bloody man, the image of death.

The apparition was not coined by Shakespeare. Its force is greater and its meaning clearer than that, for it is a traditional image from the Bible. 'Come foorth thou bloodshedder' ('man of blood' is the gloss: II Sam., 16. 7); or again, 'the Lord wyll abhorre the bloodthirstie and deceitful man' (Ps. 5, 6). Macbeth himself makes the exact verbal connection: he speaks (III. v. 126) of how augurs have 'brought forth / The secret'st *man of blood*'. We must therefore go much further than to say, with Professor Knights, that in the early part of the play the 'theme' of 'the reversal of values' is prominently 'stated'.[27] The play opens with something not static and discursive, but violent, integral to the play, and dynamic: an 'image of revolt', the image of an actual *deed* of overturning, which serves from the start as emblem both of the central character, and of the course of the action.

The double nature of Macbeth is emphasized by a turn of events at the beginning of the play which would be distracting and confusing if it did not serve exactly this purpose. This is the introduction of the Norwegian invaders, who upset Macbeth's victory over the rebel Macdonwald by their inopportune arrival. By itself, this would be wholly distracting. It is only not so, through the significance which is given to it. The new threat of danger to the state is made to underline the conflicting meanings in Macbeth's victory over the rebels. 'From that spring, whence comfort seem'd to come / Discomfort swells', says the

Sergeant (I. ii. 25): comparing the event with the coming of clouds that obscure the sun, and bring at first welcome shade, but then unwelcome storm. Both the comparison with the sun (ruler of the sky as the king is of the country), and the Sergeant's later assertion that Macbeth (and also Banquo) respond to the new challenge as if they meant to bring about 'another Golgotha' (l. 41) reinforce the effect. The Norwegians, soon forgotten, free Shakespeare to suggest, even before there is any imputation against Macbeth, that his deliverance of the state is also the opposite of a deliverance.

The nature of Macbeth's conduct, and the experience for ourselves which this makes of the play, are quite misunderstood if he is thought, however, to be an 'image of revolt' merely at the level of civil disobedience. The significance of what he does goes deeper. It must anyhow do this, if only by implication. That rebellion against the lawful king counted as rebellion against God was a commonplace of the time. The idea may be illustrated by many quotations from obvious sources such as the *Mirror for Magistrates* or the Elizabethan *Homilies*; and it simply follows, from that essential correspondence between the order of civil government and the order of nature, which (as everyone knows by now) was one of the basic ideas of Shakespeare's time, and appeared repeatedly in his work. Yet for *Macbeth*, to see this is not to see enough. It is not merely by implication that Macbeth's act of revolt is more than civic, is an ultimate revolt. It is this, clearly and with emphasis, from the start. At its inception, his plot makes his heart knock against his ribs 'against the use of nature' (I. iv. 137); Duncan on his death-bed looks 'like a breach in Nature / For Ruin's wasteful entrance' (a rich line, in which the image of Duncan himself, as bloody man, is transformed into the image of the revolt of which he is victim, and the ruin which must prove its sequel). After Banquo's ghost disrupts the feast, Macbeth thinks of how 'the secret'st man of blood' has been given away:

> Stones have been known to move, and trees to speak;
> (III. v. 123)

But the line seems to call up miracles in the past less than it suggests the anti-nature which Macbeth has created, not only in his own mind, in the present. The sense of Macbeth's career as

one of revolt against everything in the world is even sustained
by lines like those of Ross describing the woes of Scotland:

> good men's lives
> Expire before the flowers in their caps.
> Dying or ere they sicken.
>
> (IV. iii. 171)

This is no vivid Shakespearean innovation: and to find that men
are seen in it as among all the earth's other living things is merely
to hear its echoes in tradition:

Thou turnest man to destruction . . . they . . . fade away sodainly
lyke the grasse. In the morning it is greene & groweth up: but in the
evenyng it is cut downe, dryed up, and wythered.

(Ps. 90)

Again, it is no fact of disorder we are offered, but an act; one of
giant divergence whose rise and fall preoccupies the spectator
from the 'innocent flower' which Lady Macbeth tells her husband to seem like at the outset (I. v. 62), to the 'sere and yellow
leaf' into which he finds that his way (or May?) of life has fallen
in the autumn of his career. His anti-Nature has had its year,
like Nature itself.

The word 'disorder' offers no more than a vague blur in the
direction of what this anti-Nature essentially is. From the very
opening of the play, when the witches plan 'to meet with Macbeth' (I. i. 8), we have a clear clue, which may be brought into
focus by reference to Burton's catalogue of the kinds of evil
spirits:

. . . the fifth kind are cozeners, such as belong to magicians *and
witches: their prince is Satan*[28]

One after the other, and with much greater deliberateness than
Othello (*see p.* 52 *above*), Lady Macbeth and then Macbeth
dedicate themselves formally to evil, and more specifically, to
the powers of evil in traditional terms:

> Come, you spirits
> That tend on mortal thoughts, unsex me here . . .
> That no compunctious visitings of nature
> Shake my fell purpose . . .
>
> (I. v. 37)

The formalized moment of self-dedication shows as clearly here as it does in Macbeth's own prayer later:

> Now o'er the one half-world
> Nature seems dead . . .
> . . . thou sure and firm-set Earth,
> Hear not my steps . . .
>
> (II. i. 49)

But that we are to see it as dedication to the Satanic itself is reserved for a later moment, that of Macbeth's resolution to murder Banquo:

> Come seeling Night . . .
> And with thy bloody and invisible hand
> Cancel and tear to pieces that great bond
> Which keeps me pale . . .
>
> (III. ii. 46)

'bloody hand' and 'tear to pieces' resurrect, behind the words 'which keeps me pale', the recurrent apparition of the play: Macbeth's prayer is to be transformed, once for all, into the man of blood. By whose power this is to be done, is made clear in the lines which follow almost immediately:

> Good things of day begin to droop and drowse,
> While night's black agents to their preys do rouse.

In the last episode of the play, the combat between Macbeth and Macduff, it is made plain that night's black agents are the fallen angels, the powers of Satan himself:

> Despair thy charm;
> And let the *angel* which thou still hast served
> Tell thee Macduff was from his mother's womb
> Untimely ripped.
>
> (V. viii. 33)

—and also that at the end Macbeth admits, and defiantly faces, the known reward of such service:

> lay on, Macduff;
> And *damn'd* be him that first cries 'Hold, enough!'

That the rôle of the Macbeths is one of service to the principle of evil itself has one consequence which is especially important, because it recurs:

Though you untie the winds and let them fight
Against the churches; though the yesty waves
Confound and swallow navigation up;
Though bladed corn be lodg'd and trees blown down; (flattened)
Though castles topple on their warders' heads;
Though palaces and pyramids do slope
Their heads to their foundations; though the treasure
Of nature's germens tumble all together,
Even till destruction sicken—answer me
To what I ask you.

(IV. i. 52)

In these words Macbeth 'conjures' the witches (it is again, as that word suggests, a formalized speech, a recognizable and ritual act), to tell him what he needs to know, even at the cost of universal destruction. In effect, the lines come near to a curse upon the whole of Nature. Rebellion has been taken to its full extent.

There is another 'apparition' (as it might be called) besides that of the bloody man, which haunts this play, and expresses and symbolizes this aspect of Macbeth's rôle, his journey in the direction of universal chaos. It is that of riders and horses, and it seems to have gone unnoticed by critics up to now. To register the full contribution which this image makes to the play, one should call to mind something of what the armed rider, and indeed the horse itself (that almost extinct animal, at least in the *milieu* of critics) stood for in Shakespeare's society, as for millennia before. The armed rider was the surest and swiftest of all human messengers, and the signal embodiment of violence, warfare, brigandage, revolt. The horse was the most powerful and valuable of the species which served man, and at the same time, if it rebelled, the most spirited, mischievous and formidable. Both were deeply ambiguous figures, inviting admiration and fear at once.

How these images contribute to *Macbeth* becomes clearer, in fact, once their contribution to *Lear* is seen as well; but even without anticipating this feature of that play, the facts are plain enough. The oft-quoted horses of Duncan that 'turned wild in nature' and ate each other like monsters (II. iv. 14) should be seen in this light: their monstrous act is the more terrifying because it brings to life what within the world of the play is a

63

permanently latent fear. A passage from the *Homily against Wilful Rebellion* illuminates this episode. When married men revolt, it runs, they leave their wives at home, which is bad enough. It is much worse when the unmarried revolt: 'being now by rebellion set at liberty from correction of laws, they pursue other men's wives and daughters . . . *worse than any stallions or horses*'.[29] Unexpectedly perhaps for our own time, it is the horse which proves to be the obvious illustration of unbridled violence. The disturbing image runs throughout the play. The crucial scenes of the murder in Macbeth's castle at Inverness are set in the context of the arrival first of the Macbeth's messenger:

> One of my fellows had the speed of him,
> Who, almost dead for breath, had scarcely more
> Than would make up his message.
> (I. v. 32)

and then of the furiously galloping Macbeth himself:

> *Duncan:* Where's the Thane of Cawdor?
> We coursed him at the heels and had a purpose
> To be his purveyor; but he rides well,
> And his great love, sharp as his spur, hath holp him
> To his home before us.
> (I. iv. 20)

The murderers waiting for Banquo and Fleance hear their horses' hooves as they stand waiting in the dark. 'Hark, I hear horses', says the Third Murderer (III. iii. 8): and Macbeth's earlier 'I wish your horses sure and swift of foot' (III. i. 37) has made it clear that the horses (in imagination, or by theatrical device) are at a gallop. We are to envisage the same before Macbeth's last battle:

> Send out more horses, skirr the country round,
> Hang those that talk of fear
> (V. iii. 35)

and it is this sound again which Macbeth hears after his last meeting with the witches:

> Infected be the air whereon they ride;
> And damn'd all those that trust them! I did hear
> The galloping of horse. Who was't came by?
> (IV. i. 138)

What he hears, moreover (or so the spectator's impression should run), is not the presumably soundless riding away of the witches, nor merely that of the men who bring him news of Macduff's flight to England. In the last analysis, he hears also those who properly preside unseen at such a meeting; and these are the

> heaven's cherubim hors'd
> Upon the sightless couriers of the air

of his first soliloquy (I. vii. 22). Nor is the word 'hors'd' here wholly figurative: a more literal interpretation of it will bring to mind heavenly cherubim that belong to this context, and that come down from a then universally known passage of scripture:

And I sawe, and beholde, a white horse, and hee that sate on hym had a bowe, and a crowne was geuen vnto hym, and he went foorth conquering, and for to overcome. . . . And there went out another horse that was redde: and power was geuen to him that sate thereon to take peace from the earth, and that they should kyl one another. . . . And I behelde, and loe, a blacke horse: and he that sate on hym hadde a pair of ballances in his hande. . . . And I looked, and beholde a pale horse, & his name that sate on hym was death, and hel folowed with him: and power was geuen vnto them, ouer the fourth part of the earth, to kyl with sworde, & with hunger, and with dearth, and with the beastes of the earth.

(Rev. 6, 2–8)

The horses that Macbeth hears galloping are the Four Horsemen of the Apocalypse: bringing, as they ride over the earth, the disasters which are the proper result of, proper retribution for, human evil.

That the play depicts disorder spreading throughout a whole society ('bleed, bleed poor country': IV. iii. 32) is a commonplace. So is it, indeed, that this is seen as an infringement of the whole beneficent order of Nature; and that nothing less than that whole beneficent order gears itself, at last, to ending the state of evil ('. . . the pow'rs above / Put on their instruments', IV. iii. 238). That the coming of Birnam Wood to Dunsinane is a vivid emblem of this, a dumbshow of nature overturning antinature at the climax of the play, has gone unnoticed. Professor Knights once suggested that in this scene, 'nature becomes unnatural in order to rid itself of Macbeth', or rather, that it was 'emphasizing the disorder' by showing the forces of good in association with deceit and with the *un*natural.[30] To a contemporary audience, however, the scene must have presented a much more familiar and less unnatural appearance than it does to ourselves. The single figure, dressed in his distinctive costume (one should have Macbeth in his war equipment in mind) pursued by a whole company of others carrying green branches, was a familiar sight as a Maying procession, celebrating the triumph of new life over the sere and yellow leaf of winter. Herrick's *Corinna's Going a-Maying* brings out not only the gaiety of the occasion, and its intimate connections with procreation and new life even in the human sphere, but also how familiar such scenes must have been in Shakespeare's time and indeed long after:

> There's not a budding youth, or girl, this day
> But is got up, and gone to bring in May.
>   A deal of youth, ere this, is come
>   Back, and with white-thorn laden home.
> And some have wept, and wooed, and plighted troth,
>   Many a green-gown has been given
>   Many a kiss both odd and even . . .
> Many a jest told of the keys betraying
> This night, and locks picked, yet we're not a-Maying.

One should remember that the May procession, with its green branches, survived even in the London Strand until as late as the 1890s.

To a certain extent, Macbeth's career through the play almost invites being seen against the patterns of this primitive kind of ritual. Like any Lord of Misrule, he has (at least in metaphor) his ill-fitting, borrowed robes:

> now does he feel his title
> Hang loose about him, like a giant's robe
> Upon a dwarfish thief.
>   (V. ii. 20)

Moreover, he has his Feast (III. iv.) that proves only the mockery of a feast. But the interest of these details is increased, if we call to mind that there are certain features of Macbeth's career which not only fall obviously into place here, but also closely resemble moments which have already been distinguished in *Hamlet* and *Othello*. Macbeth's transition from Lord of Misrule and image of revolt to victim of the abiding and restorative forces of life is one, in fact, with that progressive isolation which (like Hamlet and Othello) he clearly undergoes. The sons of Duncan flee him, Fleance flees, Macduff

> denies his person
> At our great bidding . . .
> (III. iv. 128)

and his other followers are shams as well:

> There's not a one of them, but in his house
> I keep a servant fee'd.
> (III. iv. 131)

In the last Act, Macbeth makes his isolation explicit:

> . . . that which should accompany old age,
> As honour, love, obedience, troops of friends,
> I must not look to have.
> (V. iii. 24)

It is this scene which closes with the Doctor's profession that he too would desert if he could; and the last episode before the death of Macbeth himself is the revelation that many of his army abandoned him:

> . . . We have met with foes
> That strike beside us.
> (V. vii. 28)

Nor is our experience of merely a process whereby the protagonist is isolated. As with Othello, we are invited to recognize, and to dwell on the fact, that this journey of progressive isolation is one with its distinctive end. The protagonist, transformed bit by bit from leader to quarry, must at last stand at bay. Macbeth first registers this phase of his experience in words which resume how it was integral to it to enrol as an enemy against Nature:

> If this which he avouches does appear,
> There is *nor flying hence nor tarrying here*;
> I 'gin to be a-weary of the sun,
> *And wish th' estate o' th' world were now undone.*
> Ring the alarum bell. Blow wind, come wrack . . .
> (V. v. 47)

He confirms the coming of the final phase in a passage reminiscent of Othello's 'Here is my butt / And very sea-mark of my utmost sail':

> They have tied me to a stake; I cannot fly,
> But bear-like I must stand the course. . . .
>
> (V. vii. 1)

Nor does the resemblance end there. Macbeth's course, like Othello's, has been from man to monster. Montano's 'O monstrous act' (*Othello*, V. ii. 183) has its exact parallel in the later play; and, as in *Othello*, it comes in the closing lines, when the movement is complete, and significance at its plainest:

> *Macduff*: Then yield thee, coward,
> And live to be the gaze and show o' th' time;
> We'll have thee, *as our rarer monsters are*,
> Painted upon a pole, and underwrit,
> 'Here you may see the tyrant'.
>
> (V. viii. 26)

Finally, Malcolm in his closing speech makes clear what is at issue in the sweeping away of the dominion of the lonely monster, once he has been brought to bay and destroyed. His first thought is to re-establish the social group in all its harmonious plurality, honouring his immediate followers as earls, and

> . . . calling home our exil'd friends abroad.
>
> (V. viii. 66)

Isolation is at once to be replaced by community.

The play also moves forward in another dimension: one more intimate and inward than this of society ridding itself of its own monstrous birth, for it explores Macbeth's growing realization of what he has done. Neither in *Othello* nor in *Macbeth* is there really much question of the protagonist's repenting. In the former play, this is not because of any moral failure on Othello's part, but simply because (though many will be loth to admit it) the crucial questions of right are barely raised. Whether Montano would or should have seen Othello's act as monstrous, even had Desdemona really been confirmed in adultery, is left undiscussed. It is Iago who (in Lodovico's words) is the viper. In calling Othello merely a 'rash and most unfortunate man',

Lodovico confirms how Othello's error of *fact* is now so much
the central reality, that the moral judgement most interesting
to many in our own age is passed over. The repentance of Othello
is concentrated, like the awareness of all those with him, upon his
disastrous folly, and is not repentance in the moral sense at all.
It is quite otherwise in *Macbeth*. Here, attention is indeed concentrated on the protagonist as not foolish but fiendish. In him,
however, there is one glimpse only of something like repentance
in the full sense. It comes in the closing scene of the play, and we
should surely admire how Shakespeare held this final movement
of Macbeth's mind in reserve, sustaining our interest, insight and
sympathy at the very last:

> *Macduff:*   Turn hell-hound, turn.
> *Macbeth:* *Of all men else I have avoided thee.*
> *But get thee back; my soul is too much charged*
> *With blood of thine already.*
>
> (V. viii. 3)

Of Macbeth's genuinely beginning to turn from the evil he has
done, I can find no clear hint but this; and even this falls somewhat short of repentance proper.

On the side of intellectual response, what Macbeth comes to
recognize, and even in a limited sense regret, is his own error;
but this process of realization goes further, and takes in more,
than might be thought. Macbeth's career is an illustration, of
course, of the traditional belief, which is expressed in three
different places in scripture, that 'all they that take the sword,
shall perish with the sword' (Matth. 26, 52; cf. Gen. 9, 6, and
Rev. 13, 10). The central irony is that what Macbeth saw from
the start as a mere difficulty in his way is proved, bit by bit, to
be inescapable reality, and foreseeable as such:

> This even-handed justice
> Commends the ingredients of our poison'd chalice
> To our own lips . . .
>
> (I. vii. 10)

'From that spring whence comfort seem'd to come / Discomfort
swells' proves no truer for Duncan than it does, in turn, for
Macbeth. Two prominent speeches set the irony beyond over-
looking. The first consists in Macbeth's insincere words at the

very moment of success. He is announcing the death of Duncan, and alleging that with this, life has lost all meaning:

> Had I but died an hour before this chance
> I had lived a blessed time: for from this instant
> There's nothing serious in mortality;
> All is but toys: renown and grace is dead,
> The wine of life is drawn, and the mere lees
> Is left this vault to brag of.
>
> (II. iii. 89)

The irony goes further than the fact that, as a moral comment on what Macbeth has just done, this is more than a fitting though empty gesture, because it is the sober truth: what completes that irony is how Macbeth echoes these words, later on, in a speech as sincere as this is insincere:

Seyton: The Queen, my lord, is dead.
Macbeth: She should have died hereafter;
There would have been a time for such a word.
To-morrow, and to-morrow, and to-morrow,
Creeps in this petty pace from day to day
To the last syllable of recorded time,
And all our yesterdays have lighted fools
The way to dusty death. Out, out, brief candle!
Life's but a walking shadow, a poor player,
That struts and frets his hour upon the stage,
And then is heard no more; it is a tale
Told by an idiot, full of sound and fury,
Signifying nothing.

Whatever may be the exact relation between the first two lines of this speech and the rest, it is clear that the effect of the queen's death is to bring out finally what he has half seen before, when he says

> I am in blood
> Stepp'd in so far that, should I wade no more,
> Returning were as tedious as go o'er.

It is something which also emerges through the irony of Lady Macbeth's account of the murder:

> This night's great business . . .
> Which shall to all our nights and days to come
> Give solely sovereign sway and masterdom.
>
> (I. v. 65)

What looked as if it would endow life with the greatest mean-
ingfulness has deprived it, in the end, of all meaning. What
seemed like the beginning of everything was in fact the end of
that, and beginning of nothing. The queen's death does not
convince so much as remind Macbeth that he now knows this.
Nor, driven as he has been by both inner forces ('these terrible
dreams / That shake us nightly', III. ii. 18) and outer ('the
pow'rs above / Put on their instruments'), is this a reaction to
his personal situation alone. His cynicism is general; it is not his
own life, but Life, which has come to have no meaning.

Yet this, perhaps, falls short of the exact truth; and it perhaps
omits what is vital to the play as a whole. After all, what 'all
our yesterdays' lighted were 'fools'; and what they were lighted
to was 'dusty death'; and because of the moment when this is
said, and the fact that life is seen as one who 'struts and frets
his hour', as a tale 'full of sound and fury', it is impossible not
to see this speech as going beyond a vision of total chaos, to a
glimpse, or at least an ironical hint, of retributive order. The
fools lit to dusty death are less the innocent simpletons, than
men like Macbeth himself. His own thought has already pushed
out in this direction. The invocation to the witches was prepared
to see 'nature's germens tumble all together / *Even till Destruction
sicken*' (the passage is quoted in full on p. 63 above). Here too
Macbeth knows, or half-knows, what is fatal to his cause. That
destruction should indeed sicken is a conviction upon which the
whole movement of the play is based. When Fortune 'show'd
like a rebel's whore', it was glimpsed incompletely. Macbeth
'disdained' her too soon; just as Lady Macbeth spoke too easily
of 'Fate' having crowned her husband (I. v. 26), and Macbeth
himself spoke too easily, in inviting Fate to 'come into the list'
on his side (III. i. 70) against Banquo.

Fate, properly understood, is another kind of thing. To see
either it, or Fortune, in these ways, is like seeing only the exposed part of the iceberg. It is the injustice of Fate and Fortune
which is even-handed; their justice may come more slowly, but
in the end it redresses the balance. And if Macbeth never comes
to repent of his actions, he comes at least to comprehend not
merely that they brought him no good, but that he could have
known this, that he was wrong on a matter of fact, from the
start:

> And be these juggling fiends no more believed,
> That palter with us in a double sense,
> That keep the word of promise to our ear
> And break it to our hope.

These are his last words before his final act of animal-like
defiance. The fiends are what Burton said: cozeners; and it is a
substantial part, not only of Macbeth's response to his ordeal,
but also, and still more, of the play's whole action, that fiends
are cozeners because Fortune, or Fate, have both this surface
meaning, and their true and deeper one.

A passage from Browne's *Religio Medici* makes clear that, once
again, Shakespeare has ordered his action upon a belief basic
but familiar in his time. Saying that Nature is in effect the Art
of God, Browne writes:

> . . . this is the ordinary and open way of his Providence . . . whose
> effects we may foretel without an Oracle . . . (but) there is another
> way . . . whereof the devil and Spirits have no exact Ephemerides
> [i.e., calculating tables]; and that is a more particular and obscure
> method of his Providence, directing the operations of individuals and
> single essences: this we call *Fortune*, that serpentine and crooked
> line, whereby he draws those actions his Wisdom intends, in a more
> unknown and secret way . . . surely there are in every man's Life
> certain rubs, doublings, and wrenches, which pass a while under the
> effects of chance, but at the last, well examined, prove the meer
> hand of God . . . the lives, not only of men, but of Commonwealths,
> and the whole World, run not upon an Helix that still enlargeth, but
> on a Circle, where, arriving to their Meridian, they decline in
> obscurity, and fall under the Horizon again.
> These must not therefore be named the effects of Fortune, but in
> a relative way, and as we term the works of Nature. It was the
> ignorance of man's reason that begat this very name, and by a care-
> less term miscalled the Providence of God: for there is no liberty for
> causes to operate in a loose and stragling way.[31]

Thus *Macbeth* does not start, as does *Othello*, with something
like a plain representation of real life. Its opening scenes are
dominated less by the human figures in them, than by emblema-
tic images which embody great and indeed terrible forces running through human life, but which appear before us in detach-
ment from the realistically presented characters. Out of a world
dominated by these two images, the powers of evil in the witches,

and the emblem of revolt in the man of blood, one of the human characters emerges into prominence. At first, this is a prominence which belongs properly to the chief of the king's lieutenants and the saviour of the state.

Yet even from the start, Macbeth is more than, as it were, a plain historical figure. Through his identification with the image of revolt he becomes an icon of one of the great evil potentialities of life. Then, as it is made progressively clearer that his deed of revolt is a deliberate defiance of the whole work of Nature, and a conscious enlistment under the powers of evil, he becomes identified also with the second of these images, the 'hell-hound' of Act V scene vii: a plainer and more active embodiment of the satanic power than the witches themselves. Macbeth's status as emblem and embodiment of evil is stressed by his formal self-dedication to this as a way of life (Lady Macbeth pursues the same course), and by his ritualized invocation of universal disaster on Nature in pursuit of his own ends. His actions replace the 'bounteous nature' of the kingdom under Duncan by a condition of life which, on the level of explicit political affairs, is one of tyranny, fear, spying and continual murder; and at the level of poetic suggestion is one where ordinary life is haunted—no less emphatic word will serve—haunted by the emblematical images of the evil things of night, the armed rider, the violent horses, the Horsemen, even, of the Apocalypse. These spread through the ordinary patterns of life and give it a new quality of unnatural disruption, strangeness and violence.

As the powers of good re-assert themselves, our perspective is shifted once more. We are now invited to see Macbeth's progress through the contours, as it were, of another image, though one again which has had a long history in human thought and society. We are invited to see him as a kind of ritual victim: a scapegoat, a lord of misrule, who has turned life into riot for his limited time, and is then driven out and destroyed by the forces which embody the fertile vitality and the communal happiness of the social group. A vital part of the interest of these closing scenes is Macbeth's own growing consciousness of how what he has done futilely defies these forces, and is sterile and self-destroying.

The element of ritual in the closing scenes, their almost

imperceptible relapsing into the contours of a sacrificial fertility ceremony, the expulsion, hunting down and destruction of a man who has turned into a monster, give to the action its final shape. As the action is seen to be turning into this recognizable kind of thing, this activity which has repeatedly been a part of social life, its significance cannot but emerge into final clarity. The suspense and unpredictability which have held the audience's attention so strongly mutate into the working out of a movement which now seems pre-appointed. Macbeth is seen to have strutted and fretted his 'hour'; and both this hour, and what bring it to a close, belong to, and represent, one of the basic contours of life. Both depict for us that 'particular and obscure method of . . . Providence' through which the chaos of men's affairs is seen as reposing on an order, and the complexity and entanglement of the play to repose on an underlying form which reflects it.

V

'KING LEAR'

KING LEAR, a play set (unlike *Macbeth*) in the legendary pre-history of Britain, depicts a world which is remote and primaeval. This is not to deny that it has life and meaning for all times: its permanent relevance is what follows from having the quality of legend, and the primaeval as subject. Nor is it a merely trite observation about the play. To apprehend this fact is to be led to a decisive truth. The action of *King Lear* comprises an event which today has largely lost its meaning; though one, indeed, which points back to men's original and deepest fears and convictions, and seems to have been part of their consciousness from primitive times.

This by now largely archaic idea is present elsewhere in the tragedies. It is brought before the mind in the guards' words at the death of Antony:

> *Second Guard:*   The star is fall'n.
> *First Guard:*   *And time is at his period.*
>   (IV. xiv. 106)

It is in Macduff's words at Duncan's murder:

> Shake off this downy sleep, Death's counterfeit,
> And look on death itself. Up, up, and see
> *The great doom's image!* Malcolm! Banquo!
> *As from your graves rise up* and walk like sprites
> To countenance this horror!
>   (II. iii. 74)

The point here is that the king's end is like the end of the world: not the Day of Judgement, but the universal cataclysm which was to precede it. Twice, in *Lear*, the idea is mentioned explicitly. Kent, when he sees Lear enter with Cordelia dead in his arms, says:

> Is this the promis'd end?

and Edgar replies:

> Or image of that horror?
>
> (V. iii. 263)

The mad Lear and the blinded Gloucester meet:

> *Glou:* O, let me kiss that hand!
> *Lear:* Let me wipe it first, it smells of mortality.
> *Glou:* O ruin'd piece of nature! *This great world*
> *Shall so wear out to nought.*
>
> (IV. vi. 132)

The idea of a universal deflection of Nature towards evil and disaster (as prelude to final salvation) seems to call forth an echo elsewhere in the play. Gloucester's well-known reference to 'these late eclipses of the sun and moon' (I. ii. 99) re-echoes the words of St Luke on the end of the world:

And there shalbe signes in the Sunne, and in the Moone, & in the starres; and upon the earth trouble among the nations, with perplexitie, the sea and the water roring: And mens hartes fayling them for feare, and for looking after those thinges which are comming on the worlde: for the powers of heaven shalbe shaken.

> (21. 25-6)

The storm on the heath recalls what the Book of Revelation says of Armageddon:

And there folowed voyces, thundringes, and lightnynges: and there was a great earthquake, such as was not since men were upon the earth . . .

> (16. 18)

For the Elizabethans, the End of the World was a living conviction and even something of a current fear. We touch here on one of the oldest of traditions: that notion of the world's turning upside down which Archilochus already employs when, having unexpectedly seen an eclipse of the sun, he says that the fish might as well now come and feed on land, or wolves feed in the sea. Repeated incessantly,[32] by Shakespeare's time this was a long-established commonplace; but when Hooker (though merely adapting Arnobius) finds his imagination kindled by this thought, and turns from detailed analysis to write with the full range of his eloquence, the idea is present in all its power and solemnity:

Now if nature should intermit her course . . . if those principal and mother elements of the world . . . should lose the qualities which they now have; if the frame of that heavenly arch erected over our heads should loosen and dissolve itself; if celestial spheres should forget their wonted motions . . . if the moon should wander from her beaten way, the times and seasons of the year blend themselves by disordered and confused mixture, the winds breathe out their last gasp, the clouds yield no rain, the earth be defeated of heavenly influence, the fruits of the earth pine away as children at the withered breasts of their mother no longer able to yield them relief; what then would become of man himself?[33]

The reader of Shakespeare has thus to recognize that the 'Elizabethan World Picture' pictured an order quite different from anything which would now come to mind as order. Coherent and providential system as it was, it included within itself a standing potentiality for progressive transformation into chaos. Paradoxically, the more that the world is conceived in religious terms, the easier is it for a potentiality of deflection into chaos to stand as no radical infringement, but a genuine ingredient of order. Further than this, for Shakespeare's time collapse into universal chaos was not merely a permanent possibility in a fallen (though divinely created) Nature: it was a foreordained part of created Nature's route to salvation; and to envisage it, to dwell on it, to comprehend what it could be like, was part of what went to make up a comprehension of God's governance of the world.

How *Lear* is in part a rehearsal of this terrible potentiality of Nature becomes plainer, if one bears in mind that what the descent into chaos would be like was delineated by tradition. It already had its familiar contours and features. There is no need here to do more than hint briefly at the length and strength of this tradition. If we go back, for example, to Mark 13, which is the chapter in that gospel corresponding to Luke 21 (the account of the final calamity of the world which was briefly quoted above) we see the major concerns of *Lear* emerge one by one: 'There shal nation rise against nation, & kingdome against kingdome: and there shalbe earthquakes . . . the brother shall betray the brother to death, and the father the sonne: and the children shal rise against their fathers and mothers, and shal put them to death.' From this one might turn to Wulfstan's *Sermon to the English People*, composed in response to the chaos over-taking England when the Danish invasion was at its height: '. . . the father did not stand by his child, nor the child by the father, nor one brother by another . . .' and—sign of the tradi-tional combination of ideas from which Lear itself emerged—Wulfstan goes on immediately to speak of how treachery, un-lawfulness and infidelity to one's lord have spread everywhere throughout the land.[34]

What must have been a passage familiar to all of Shakespeare's audience, the Homily of 1574 *Against Disobedient and Wilful Rebellion*, also clearly sees dissension between parents and children as the predictable counterpart of dissension in the body politic: 'when the subjects unnaturally do rebel against their prince . . . countrymen to disturb the public peace and quiet-ness of their country, for defence of whose quietness they should spend their lives: the brother to seek, and often to work the death of his brother; the son of the father, the father to seek or procure the death of his sons, being at man's age, and by their faults to disherit their innocent children. . . .'[35] Donne's well-known reference to how 'new philosophy calls all in doubt' in the First Anniversary belongs to the same train of thought. These words, so often quoted in bleak and misleading isolation, easily misrepresent the main weight of Donne's argument. This by no means expresses a new-found disquiet resulting from new astronomy or anything like it. All that such things do for Donne is provide mere topical confirmation of that fallen condition which is established on other grounds and by the longest of traditions.

> Then, as mankinde, so is the worlds whole frame
> Quite out of joynt, *almost created lame*:
> For, before God had made up all the rest,
> Corruption entred, and deprav'd the best:
> It seis'd the Angels . . .
> The noblest part, man, felt it first; and then
> Both beasts and plants, curst in the curse of man.
> *So did the world from the first houre decay.* . . .

Here is the beginning of Donne's discussion. The reference to 'new philosophy' has a subordinate place in the middle of it. The poet goes straight on to rehearse the traditional counterparts of chaos in Nature (counterparts, needless to say, having nothing to do with 'new philosophy'), and these take us straight back to *Lear*:

> 'Tis all in peeces, all cohaerence gone;
> All just supply, and all Relation:
> *Prince, Subject, Father, Sonne are things forgot,*
> For every man alone thinkes he hath got
> To be a Phoenix, and that then can bee
> None of that kinde, of which he is, but hee . . .

Finally, a passage from Burton's *Anatomy of Melancholy*, resuming the same point, also relates it directly to the twin threads of action which run through the movement of the play: 'Great affinity is there is betwixt a political and an economic body [i.e. a house or family]; they differ only in magnitude; *as they have both likely the same period* . . . six or seven hundred years, so many times they have the same means of their vexation and overthrow; as namely riot, a common ruin of both.' [36]

Disruption in the kingdom, disruption in the family, linked by tradition, were facets of that universal disruption of Nature, that Descent into Chaos, which for millennia had been a standing dread of mankind and at the same time one of mankind's convictions about providential history in the future.

King Lear is an exploration of this potentiality to quite a different degree from, say, *Macbeth*. The nadir of that play, the point at which Macbeth's own evil nature seems to diffuse evil throughout his whole country, falls short of what happens even at the very start of *Lear*. In *Macbeth* the evil emanates from one man (or one couple) quite alone. In *Lear* it seems, from the first, like an infection spreading everywhere, affecting a general change in human nature, even in all nature. Those, like Kent and Cordelia, who stand out against its progress, manifest its influence even in doing so: as if Burton's 'riot' could be countered (which may be true, indeed) only by riot of another kind. The disease is general; antidotes are helpless or non-existent; the course must be run.

In its details, the play sometimes displays an extraordinary realism. Lear's hesitation before he demands to see the supposedly sick Duke of Cornwall and his inability to believe that his messenger has been set in the stocks, Edgar's impersonation of the peasant, the whole dialogue in Act V scene iii between Albany, Edmund, Goneril and Regan, are all instances of unforgettable rightness and richness in catching the complex and individualized movements of minds vehemently working and intently engaged. Yet for a sense of the play as a whole this has less weight than what is almost its opposite: an action deliberately stylized so that its generic quality and its decisive movement should stand out more than its human detail. This is true, notably, of the division of the kingdom with which the play opens. We must see this as stylized not merely in its quality as it takes place on the stage, but in how it points forward. Time and again this kind of event occurs in contemporary drama (*Gorboduc, The Misfortunes of Arthur, Selimus, Woodstock, Locrine* are examples). Its status as decisively misguided or evil is not in doubt; and it is the established sign or first step in a movement which threatens chaos or actually brings it. The direction and nature of what is to happen in *Lear* need not be inferred by the spectator through his detailed response to the behaviour and dialogue of the actors. Richly as it may be confirmed and elaborated in these things, its essence stands starkly before him in the stylization of a known kind of opening event. The intricate complication of the story, the detailed characterization, do nothing to obscure what is clear in the almost folk-tale quality of how the play begins. '*We have seen* the best of our time.'

Those words of Gloucester are essentially dynamic words, and this movement and dynamic ought to be seen in an aspect of *King Lear* which has been so much discussed that here it need not be discussed in full: its imagery. That the characters in the play are repeatedly likened to the lower orders of creation, for example, gives no mere general or pervasive tinge to the work, and embodies no merely general idea about humanity at large. It cannot be found in the opening scene. It arrives as the action begins to move, and becomes dominant as the quality of life which it embodies becomes dominant in the play. Just as it is not enough for Professor Muir to say that the plot of Lear 'expressed the theme of the parent–child relationship'—for it expressed no mere problem or issue, because it depicts a parti-

cular movement which begins when that relationship fails in a
definite way—so it is not enough for him to refer to 'the preva-
lence of animal imagery' and to add merely: 'This imagery is
partly designed to show man's place in the Chain of Being, and
to bring out the subhuman nature of the evil characters, partly
to show man's weakness compared with the animals, and partly
to compare human life to the life of the jungle.'[37] The hedge-
sparrow that fed the cuckoo, the sea-monster that is less hideous
than ingratitude in a child, ingratitude itself sharper than a
serpent's tooth, the wolfish visage of Goneril, are not scattered
through the play as mere figurative embodiments of those discursive or philosophical interests. They burst upon the audience
all together, at the close of Act I. If they throw out some
general and discursive suggestion about 'human life', that is far
less prominent than how they qualify the phase of the action
which comes at that point, crowding the audience's imagination,
surrounding the human characters with the subhuman creatures whose appearance they are fast and eagerly assuming.

Likewise, when Kent (II. ii. 67–89) speaks of the rats 'that
bite the holy cords atwain', and the men who follow their
masters like ignorant dogs or are no different from cackling
geese, we are offered no general comment upon human life, but
a context in imagery for the conduct of Oswald which preoccupies here and now. The society of the play, in its descent
into animality, had reached this point. Edgar, shortly after,
underlines the change going on before our eyes:

> I will preserve myself; and am bethought
> To take the basest and most poorest shape
> That ever penury in contempt of man
> *Brought near to beast.*
>
> (II. iii. 6)

The descent continues; Regan, Cornwall, Gloucester and Edgar
are all drawn in as its ministers or its victims; and now the
images gain a new quality. They do indeed become general, for
the disease they reflect and stress has become general. The play
is indeed coming to depict, in Hooker's phrase, an earth
'defeated of heavenly influence'; and the Fool's

Horses are tied by the heads, dogs and bears by th' neck, monkeys
by th' loins, and *men* by the legs . . .

(II. iv. 7)

underlines this. 'Man's life is cheap as beast's', Lear adds a moment later (II. iv. 266).

All this is enforced by the progressive transformation, as Act II advances, of the settled society of men, with their fixed abodes, into a confusion of people constantly leaving their homes, constantly on horseback and riding recklessly from place to place. Lear's own words, towards the close of this movement, make the point of it:

> They have travelled all the night! Mere fetches!
> *The images of revolt and flying off.*
>
> (II. iv. 87)

Yet Lear himself, quitting Goneril, is the first to break with the settled order:

> . . . Darkness and devils!
> Saddle my horses; call my train together.
>
> . . . Prepare my horses.
>
> . . . Go, go, my people.
>
> . . . Away, away!
> (I. iv. 251–2, 258, 272, 289)

Goneril, in the person of her messengers, is quick to follow his example:

> Take you some company, and away to horse . . .
> (I. iv. 337)

Next, it is Cornwall of whom Edmund, at his father's castle, says:

> He's coming hither now, *i' th' night, i' th' haste*,
> And Regan with him.
>
> (II. i. 24)

And Kent explains that this hurried journey was the immediate result, like the spreading of an infection, of a letter from Goneril:

> . . . Which presently they read; on whose contents
> They summoned up their meiny, straight took horse,
> Commanded me to follow . . .
>
> (II. iv. 33)

Regan has already set the tone of her journey more fully than she intended:

> *Cornwall:* You know not why we came to visit you.
> *Regan:* Thus *out of season, threading dark-eyed night.*
> (II. ii. 118)

The last appearance of this motif of the horse and the homeless rider comes once again from Lear himself:

> *Glo:* The king is in high rage.
> *Corn:* Whither is he going?
> *Glo:* He calls to horse; but will I know not whither . . .
> Alack, the night comes on, and the high winds
> Do sorely ruffle; for many miles about
> There's scarce a bush.

Nothing could lead on more clearly to the idea that the society of men is becoming the chaotic world of the outlaw.

This descent from humanity, however, is something which cannot be envisaged fully through the idea of the brute and its animal life alone. It is a descent, embodied in the action, enriched by imagery, and confirmed by what is said as comment, far below brutality. Lear does not only 'choose . . . To be a comrade of with the wolf and owl' (II. iv. 207). He sinks lower still: recreant against Nature and outcast among its creatures:

> This night, wherein the cub-drawn bear would crouch,
> The lion, and the belly-pinched wolf
> Keep their fur dry, unbonneted he runs,
> And *bids what will* take all.
> (III. i. 12)

Edgar joins him ('What art thou that dost grumble there i' th' straw?' asks Kent, III. iv. 43). The spectacle is of man below the animals, since he combines the vices of all of men in his single self:

> Hog in sloth, fox in stealth, wolf in greediness, dog in madness, lion in prey . . .
> (III. iv. 91)

It is only now, when all left of humanity seems to be a madman, a beggar and a jester surrounded by the storm, that the extreme is reached, and the thought of it put forward at last:

Lear: Why, thou wert better in a grave than to answer with thy
uncover'd body this extremity of the skies. Is man no more
than this? Consider him well.

[this 'him' means Edgar as much as man in general]

Thou ow'st the worm no silk, the beast no hide, the sheep no
wool, the cat no perfume. Here's three on us are sophisticated!
Thou are the thing itself: unaccommodated man is no more
but such a poor, bare, forked animal as thou art. Come, off,
you lendings! Come, unbutton here.

(III. iv. 100)

Regan and Goneril also seem to pass down through, and out
of, the whole order of Nature; though they are its monsters not
its remnants. The word itself, already recurrent in the present
discussion, is explicitly used of each of them (III. vii. 101;
IV. ii. 62–3); and Albany, in two of the comments which he
makes about his wife, draws attention not only to the kind of
movement which the play has displayed so far, but also—and it
is an important new point—to that further movement with
which it will close. He asserts that what has happened so far is
bringing his society (again the stress is upon the movement,
upon its being *brought*) to the condition of the sea, with its
universal war, unlimited in savagery, of all against all:

If that the heavens do not their visible spirits
Send quickly down to tame these vile offences,
It will come
Humanity must perforce prey on itself,
Like monsters of the deep.

(IV. ii. 46)

Besides this, he indicates what may be expected to ensue:

That nature which condemns it origin
Cannot be border'd certain in itself;
She that herself will sliver and disbranch
From her material sap, perforce must wither
And come to deadly use . . .

(IV. ii. 32)

The thought is near to that of Cornwall's servants:

Second Serv: I'll never care what wickedness I do
If this man come to good.

Third Serv: If she live long,
                 And in the end meet the old course of death,
                 Women will all turn monsters.
                                    (III. vii. 98)

Lear's part in this change is a special one. He is not only the
'slave' of the elements; he is also the man to whom Kent said
'. . . you have that in your countenance that I would fain call
master . . . authority' (I. iv. 27). But his special part is best
understood by dwelling upon something which has seldom
received much attention: the clear parallel (though it is also a
clearly limited one) between the condition of Lear, and that in
the Old Testament of Job. This follows on naturally from how
the play brings men down to animals, because Gloucester's
'I' th' last night's storm I such a fellow saw / Which made me
think a man a worm' (IV. i. 33), recalls Job's 'I sayde . . . to
the wormes, You are my mother, and my syster' (17, 14). Again,
Albany's 'O Goneril! / You art not worth the dust which the
rude wind / Blows in your face' sees Goneril as less than the dust,
and thus echoes a thought constant in *Job*: 'nowe must I sleepe
in the dust'; 'Thou madest me as the mould of the earth, and
shalt bring me into dust agayne'; 'our rest together is in the
dust'; 'one dyeth in his ful strength . . . another dyeth in the
bitternesse of his soule . . . they shal sleepe both alike in the
earth and the wormes shal cover them'; 'all fleshe shall come
to nought at once, and al men shal turne agayne unto dust'
(7, 21; 10, 9; 21, 23–6; 34, 15).
    Yet these two points are merely the beginning of a much
wider resemblance. Job's patience is something that Lear early
claims for himself (II. iv. 229; cf. 'I will be the pattern of all
patience'; (III. ii. 37), and that Gloucester ultimately acquires:

                    henceforth I'll bear
            Affliction till it do cry out itself
            'Enough, enough,' and die.
                        (IV. vi. 75)

There are many other links in matters, comparatively speaking,
of detail. 'Thou puttest my fete also in the stockes' (13, 27); 'for
the vehemencie of sorowe is my garment changed, which com-
passeth me about as the coller of my coat' (30, 18; cf. 'come,
unbutton here', III. iv. 106; and 'pray you undo this button',

V. iii. 309); 'Wherefore do wycked men liue, come to theyr olde
age, and encrese in ryches' (21, 7; cf. 'Is there any cause in
nature that makes these hard hearts', III. vi. 76, and the ser-
vant's '. . . if she live long, / And in the end meet the old course
of death . . .', III. vii. 99).

Besides these sharp if local resemblances, there are passages
in *Job* that seem to resume whole sections of the play: 'They
cause the poore to turne out of the way . . . they cause the
naked to lodge wythout garment and wythout coveryng in the
colde. They are wet wyth the showres of the mountaynes, and
embrace the rocks for want of a covering' (24. 4–8). 'Heare then
the sound of his voice, & the noyse that goeth out of his mouth.
He directeth it under the whole heaven, and his lyght [= light-
ning] unto the endes of y^e world. A roryng voyce foloweth . . .
thundreth marveylously wyth his voyce . . . He commandeth
the snow, and it falleth upon earth: he geueth the rayne a
charge, & the shouers have their strength and fal downe'
(37. 2–6). Finally (though it still remains, to discuss exactly
what light these parallels throw) in one passage Lear's whole
situation is summed up: 'Myne owne kinsfolkes haue forsaken
me and my best acquaynted haue forgotten me. The seruantes
and maydes of myne owne house tooke me for a stranger, and
I am become as an aliant [= alien] in theyr sight. I called my
seruant, and he gaue me no answere . . . Al my most familiers
abhorred me: and they whome I loued best are turned agaynst
me' (19. 14–18).

A resemblance, even a massive resemblance such as exists
here, is one thing; light thrown on the exact contour of *King
Lear* is another. Yet light is certainly thrown, and abundantly.
How this is so may perhaps best be seen through taking note
of something both plain and remarkable about the action of
the play: what might be called not its *action*, but its *protraction*.
In one sense, *Lear* is a much longer play than it need have been
—need have been, that is, to have been less ambitiously tragic.
By the middle of Act IV (or even the end of Act III) something
of an ordinary tragic action has been completed. Lear has fallen
from being the minion of Fortune (when the play opens he is
presented as in one sense a king of kings) to being its chief
victim. Through the ordeal of this fall, his eyes have been
opened. From being one who 'hath ever but slenderly known

86

himself' (I. i. 292), he has come to say 'Here I stand your slave, / A poor infirm, weak and despised old man' (III. ii. 19). He has learnt, moreover, or re-learnt, the central and traditional lessons that good kings must know:

> Poor naked wretches, wheresoe'er you are,
> That bide the pelting of this pitiless storm,
> How shall your houseless heads and unfed sides,
> Your loop'd and window'd raggedness, defend you
> From seasons such as these? O, I have ta'en
> Too little care of this! Take physic, pomp;
> Expose thyself to feel what wretches feel. . . .
>
> (III. iv. 28)

The lines express something of what Piers Plowman learns from Hunger,[38] and the facts to which they point are those explicit in the Wakefield *Second Shepherd's Play*, and implicit indeed in the *Magnificat*. The twin passages which begin:

> Tremble, thou wretch
> That hast within thee undivulged crimes
> Unwhipped of justice . . .
>
> (III. ii. 51)

and

> Thou rascal beadle, hold thy bloody hand.
> Why dost thou lash that whore? Strip thy own back;
> Thou hotly lusts to use her in that kind
> For which thou whip'st her . . .
>
> (IV. vi. 160)

are not well seen as philosophical passages about appearance and reality. Their import is moral. They are conventional and traditional, their power lying in this very embodiment of the familiar facts of human hypocrisy in all their brutal force and immediacy; and their point of origin is St Paul: '. . . Thou therfore which teachest another, teachest thou not thy selfe? thou that preachest, A man should not steale, doest thou steale? Thou that sayest, A man should not commit adulterie, doest thou commit adultery? thou that abhorrest idoles, committest thou sacriledge? Thou that gloriest in the Lawe, through breaking the Law dishonourest thou God . . . ?' (Romans 2, 21–3). Moreover, Lear had learned to repent: '. . . these things sting /

His mind so venomously that burning shame / Detains him from Cordelia' (IV. iv. 45); and by the end of Act IV it partly seems that his madness has ceased: 'Be comforted, good madam. The great rage, / You see, is killed in him' (IV. iv. 78).

The completeness of this change must not be insisted on beyond a certain point (though that there is something of the same kind in Gloucester's situation seems clear enough). A transition from blindness and injustice, through suffering, to self-knowledge, responsibility and repentance, is not the final import even of this long central section of the play. Nevertheless, it is there plainly enough. The materials exist for a more conventional and less protracted tragedy which could have ended well before the beginning of Act V. If we ask what extends the play further, the Book of Job reveals the answer.

What makes the situation of Job unique may be brought out by starting from the position of Job's comforters: Eliphaz's 'Who ever perished being an innocent? or where were the upright destroyed (4, 7), and Bildad's 'if thou be pure and upright, then surely he wil awake up unto thee' (8, 6). The comforters are orthodox. The men God punishes are sinners. Those who live piously under affliction, he restores; and so far as they are concerned, the sinister implications in Job's case are plain enough. But Job's protracted afflictions are a challenge to this orderly and consoling doctrine. When, despite his miseries, he 'holdeth fast to his integrity' ('In all this Job sinned not') his miseries are simply re-doubled. This is the extraordinary event, the terrifying paradox indeed, which begins and demands the discussion that occupies the rest of the work. If there is any order of Nature at all, good must now replace evil; instead, evil returns twofold and is prolonged far beyond its proper span.

The action of *Lear* is also prolonged by this same conception. Repeatedly, we are made to think that since Nature is an order (though doubtless a stern one) release from suffering is at hand; but instead, the suffering is renewed. Act IV, the Act in which the play takes on its second and more remarkable lease of life, conspicuously begins with this very turn of thought and situation. Edgar, seeing himself at the very bottom of Fortune's wheel, finds cause for hope (living as he thinks in a world of order) in that fact alone:

> To be worst,
> The lowest and most dejected thing of fortune,
> Stands still in esperance, lives not in fear.
> The lamentable change is from the best;
> The worst returns to laughter. Welcome, then,
> Thou unsubstantial air that I embrace!
> (IV. i. 2)

At this very moment, he encounters his father and sees that he has been blinded; and his response is to recognize the very potentiality of life which was embodied in the story of Job:

> O gods! Who is't can say 'I am at the worst'?
> I am worse than e'er I was . . .
> And worse I may be yet. The worst is not
> So long as we can say 'This is the worst'.
> (IV. i. 26)

The bitter reversal of events comes again and again. It is less than the full truth to say (as was suggested on p. 88) that Lear recovers from his madness during Act IV. The 'great rage' may be killed in him, but among his first words to Cordelia, when he is awakened out of sleep and we hope momentarily for his recovery, are:

> If you have poison for me, I will drink it.
> (IV. vii. 72)

Cordelia's army, coming to rescue her father, succeeds only in putting her as well as him into the hands of their worst enemies. Later it seems as if Lear and Cordelia are to find a kind of private happiness in prison together. Yet even as this vision forms in our minds, we recall Edmund's threat, and realize that

> The good years shall devour them, flesh and fell,
> Ere they shall make us weep . . .
> (V. iii. 24)

is hopeless fantasy on Lear's part, and only too soon to be proved so. Later still, the threat appears to be removed; for as he is dying Edmund confesses to his plot, and the Captain is sent hurrying to save Cordelia from death. But again, we are worse than e'er we were: the only result, the immediate result, is Lear's entry with Cordelia in his arms.

Perhaps this ironic turn in events, this constant intensifying
of disaster at the moment when disaster seems to be over, is
represented yet once again in the play: in the very moment of
Lear's death. Conceivably, Lear is meant to think for a moment
that Cordelia is alive; and dies before he realizes his mistake.
Certainly, our hopes for Lear himself are, in a limited sense,
raised once more by the words of Albany which immediately
precede Lear's last speech. On either or both these counts, it
seems as if some kind of remission is at hand; but at this moment
Lear suffers the last infliction of all. Nor is it possible to accept,
as true in anything but an incomplete and strained sense, R. W.
Chambers' opinion that both Lear and Gloucester 'die of joy'.[39]
Edgar has already given the audience the exact truth of
Gloucester's death:

> But his flaw'd heart—
> Alack, too weak the conflict to support!—
> 'Twixt two extremes of passion, joy and grief,
> Burst smilingly.
>
> (V. iii. 196)

The last two words confirm a paradoxical combination of joy
and grief, they do not convert it to a state of bliss; and it is a
somewhat bold interpretation of the moment of Lear's death,
one which without the parallel to Gloucester (and perhaps with
it) would be over-bold, to assert that there, joy lies even in
equal balance with grief. That Lear's heart breaks is clear from
the words of Kent ('Break heart, I prithee break'); and that this
is the culmination of an ordeal of torment renewed almost
beyond belief, is what we are instructed to see by what this
reliable authority says next:

> Vex not his ghost. O, let him pass! He hates him
> That would *upon the rack* of this rough world
> Stretch him out longer.
>
> (V. iii. 312)

This in fact is the note sounded throughout the closing scenes.
The world can be to mankind, and has been to Lear, a rack: a
scene of suffering reiterated past all probability or reason. It
can be a place of which Edgar was able to say, at the beginning
of Act IV:

World, world, O world!
But that thy strange mutations make us hate thee,
Life would not yield to age.

(IV. i. 10)

Later, only a few moments before the play closes, he goes on
from the account of his father's death to hint plainly at the
coming death of Kent:

Edmund: . . . but speak you on;
                You look as you had something more to say.
Albany: If there be more, more woeful, hold it in;
                For I am almost ready to dissolve,
                Hearing of this.
Edgar: This would have seem'd a period
                To such as love not sorrow; but another,
                To amplify too much, would make much more,
                And *top extremity*.
                While I was big in clamour, came there in a man . . .
                . . . His grief grew puissant, and the strings of life
                Began to crack.

This is to underline once more the idiom of the play's later
movement, its reiteration of suffering, to 'top extremity', when
it seems that suffering must surely be over.

At this stage in the discussion, one must try to record the note
upon which *King Lear* is resolved. It is not easy to do so, and it is
less easy than more than one distinguished critic has allowed.
One interpretation, certainly, has attracted many readers. We
may frame it, with Professor Chambers, as 'the victory of Cordelia and of Love'; or with Professor Knights, as the 'complete
endorsement of love as a quality of being', or with Professor
Wilson Knight, as 'the primary persons, good and bad, die
into love'.[40] It is better to see the play thus, than to regard its
close as the embodiment only of cynicism, chaos and despair.
But one should remind oneself at this point of what, surely, is
familiar knowledge: that love (unless that word is taken, as
I fear it is often taken, to mean every good thing) is a value
with a great but finite place in human life; and that if it is a
full description of the affirmation on which the play closes, that
affirmation is a limited one; is indeed, curiously inadequate,
curiously out of scale with the range, power and variety of the
issues of life on which this incomparable work has touched.

Those for whom the word 'love' is a talisman will find this suggestion objectionable. That may be an argument in its favour.

With these considerations in mind, one may incline to see the close of *Lear* in another light. The survivors of Cleopatra, say, and of Brutus and Coriolanus, indeed speak as though these characters enjoyed a kind of victory or triumph even in death. When, at the close of *Lear*, Shakespeare characteristically gives those who survive the protagonist lines which suggest what the audience is to see in his end, it is not to any victory or triumph, through love or anything else, that he makes them direct our attention. He causes them to agree that there has never been such a case of a man stretched out on the rack of the world, and released at last. At the close of *Macbeth* there is much emphasis on a movement of regeneration, a restoration of good at the level of the body politic. Lear ends more sombrely. 'Our present business . . . is general woe', says Albany, appealing to Kent and Edgar for nothing more optimistic than to help him rule and 'the *gor'd* state *sustain*'—the modest ambition of that last word should not be missed. The last speech of all, that of Edgar, seems peculiarly significant, for all its bald rhyming:

> The weight of this sad time we must obey:
> *Speak what we feel, not what we ought to say,*
> The oldest hath borne most; *we that are young*
> *Shall never see so much nor live so long.*

The ordeal has been unique in its protraction of torment, and the note is surely one of refusal to hide that from oneself, refusal to allow the terrible potentialities of life which the action has revealed to be concealed once more behind the veil of orthodoxy and the order of Nature. If there is such an order, it is an order which can accommodate seemingly limitless chaos and evil. The play is a confrontation of that, a refusal to avert one's gaze from that. Its affirmation is as exalted, humane and life-affirming as affirmation can be, for it lies in a noble and unflinching steadiness, where flinching seems inevitable, in the insight of its creator.

To turn to a more intimate awareness of the personal bonds on which the play closes is to extend and amplify this, and still to see something other than what deserves the name of 'love' *tout court*. Perhaps there is a clue in the fact that it is Edmund

('Yet Edmund was beloved', V. iii. 239) and only Edmund, who speaks of love by itself. We are meant, of course, to see it as embodied always in what Cordelia does; but in her sole reference to this in the later scenes of the play, what she at once goes on to speak of is not her love but, in effect, her duty:

> No blown ambition does both our arms incite,
> But love, dear love, *and our ag'd father's right*.
>
> (IV. iv. 26)

This stress, not on loving alone, but on doing and being what it falls to one to do and be, is so insistent that its having been left unregarded is surprising. Cordelia's first speech of any substance to the re-awakened Lear confirms its relevance for both her and him:

> O look upon me, sir,
> And hold your hands in benediction o'er me.
> No, sir, you must not kneel.
>
> (IV. vii. 57)

What she wants is for him to do what it is a father's duty to do: not what it is *her* duty to do in return. The same kind of thought is prominent in Lear's first speech after capture:

> When thou dost ask me blessing, I'll kneel down,
> And ask of thee forgiveness.
>
> (V. iii. 10)

Each of them is to do what (paradoxically, in Lear's case) it is appropriate for them to do: the idea is of service and duteousness, not love in any simple or emotional sense. In just this light, too, are we invited to see Edgar's bond with his father:

> *Albany:* How have you known the miseries of your father?
> *Edgar:* By nursing them, my Lord . . .
>   . . . became his guide,
> Led him, begg'd for him, sav'd him from despair;
> Never—O fault!—reveal'd myself unto him
> Until some half-hour past, when I was arm'd;
> Not sure, though hoping, of this good success,
> I asked his blessing, and from first to last
> Told him my pilgrimage.
>
> (V. iii. 180–96)

Kent's devotion to Lear is of course one in which feeling means service:

> I am the very man . . .
> That from your first of difference and decay
> Have followed your sad steps.
> (V. iii. 285)

> I have a journey, sir, shortly to go.
> My master calls me; I must not say no.
> (V. iii. 321)

The bond which remains, at the play's close, among the other (or perhaps only) survivors, is of the same kind:

> *Albany:*   . . . Friends of my soul, you twain
> Rule in this realm, and the gor'd state sustain.
> (V. vii. 319)

With these many pointers in mind, perhaps the final import of the reconciliation of Lear to Cordelia, or Gloucester to Edgar, may also be seen as meaning more than the word 'love' can easily mean, at least in our own time; and as being, in the end, one with the whole of what happens at the close of the drama. That the closing phase is one in which the evil in the play proves self-destructive, is well known. Evil has come, it has taken possession of the world of the play, it has brought men below the level of the beasts, it has destroyed itself, and it has passed. Good (I have argued) is far from enjoying a triumphant restoration: we are left with the spectacle of how suffering can renew itself unremittingly until the very moment of death.

If, at the close, some note less despairing than this may be heard, it comes through our apprehending that in an austere and minimal sense, Edmund's words 'the wheel has come full circle' extend, despite everything, beyond himself. Below the spectacle of suffering everywhere in possession, is another, inconspicuous but genuine: that the forces of life have been persistently terrible and cruel, but have also brought men back to do the things it is their part to do. Union with Cordelia barely proves Lear's salvation: his salvation is what Kent says, release from a life of torment. But that union is the thing to which he rightly belongs. He deviated from it, and life itself brought him back. So with Gloucester. To follow the master, to sustain the state, to bless one's child, to succour the aged and one's parents —this idea of being brought back to rectitude is what the play ends with. These are the things which it falls to living men to do; and if the play advances a 'positive', I think it is that when men turn away from how they should live, there are forces in life which constrain them to return. In this play, love is not a 'victory'; it is not that which stands at 'the centre of the action', and without which 'life is meaningless'; it does not rule creation. If anything rules creation, it is (though only, as it were, by a hairsbreadth) simply rule itself. What order restores, is order. Men tangle their lives; life, at a price, is self-untangling at last.

In view of these things, how fantastic it would be to call *King Lear* a play of intrigue! Yet this idea, immediate though its rejection must be, does indeed suggest the many things going on, and being intricately fitted together, which mark the closing scenes of the play. This very fact is what leads back from the attitudes of the play to what is more intimate with its substance, and with the experience which it offers to us in its sequence. The war with France, the intrigue between Edmund and the sisters, the emergence of Albany, Edmund's plot with the captain and his duel with Edgar, densen into a medium of something like quotidian life, through which and beyond which Lear's own situation stands out in isolation. It is the very variety in the strands of life which brings out how, at the end, life as it were stands back from Lear; and affords him a remoteness, a separation from his fellows, in which his ordeal is completed.

This is the culmination, moreover, of how he begins. As in the tragedies which have been discussed already, at the outset the protagonist is at the focal point of all men's regard. But Lear's progressive isolation does not steal upon him, or his audience, unawares. Relinquishing the kingdom, repudiating Cordelia, banishing Kent, cursing Goneril (I. iv. 275–289), departing wrathfully from Regan:

> He calls to horse, and will I know not whither . . .
> (II. iv. 296)

—all these actions set Lear, of his own free will, apart from his fellows; and are the prelude to how he sets himself apart, first from human contact of any kind whatsoever:

> No, rather I abjure all roofs, and choose
> To wage against the enmity o' th' air . . .
> (II. iv. 207)

and then from the whole of Nature:

> This night, wherein the cub-drawn bear would crouch,
> The lion, and the belly-pinched wolf
> Keep their fur dry, unbonneted he runs,
> And *bids what will take all.*
>
> (III. i. 12)

Yet Lear's position is ambiguous. In his first speech on the heath he is not only the almost satanic enemy of Nature, cursing it in its entirety; but also its victim.

> Strike flat the thick rotundity o' th' world
> Crack nature's moulds, all germens spill at once,
> That make ingrateful man. . . .
>
> (III. ii. 7)

is followed almost at once by:

> . . . Here I stand, your slave,
> A poor, infirm, weak and despis'd old man.

If the tenor of the first passage is unmistakably like that of Macbeth's giant defiance ('though the treasure / Of nature's germens tumble all together / Even till destruction sicken— answer me / To what I ask you . . .'), the second has its counterpart in *Macbeth* as well. Macbeth's 'They have tied me to a stake; I cannot fly' has its closest parallel, indeed, in Gloucester's 'I am tied to the stake, and I must stand the course' (III. vii. 53); but if Gloucester is like Macbeth in that his fate is more of an execution than anything else, so is Lear. Kent's thought of him on the rack is a variant of his own

> I am bound
> Upon a wheel of fire, that mine own tears
> Do scald like molten lead.
>
> (IV. vii. 46)

The parallel with Macbeth is a strange and clear one; and the full currency in Shakespeare's own mind of the image through which we see the king in the later part of the play must be brought to attention and life. Today, the direction 'enter Lear, fantastically dressed with weeds' can easily seem mere fantasy without a background, or have merely some kind of enrichment in generalized associations with fertility and its converse. For

Shakespeare, Lear's status in this scene must have been much more exact and significant. The figure

> Crown'd with rank fumiter and furrow weeds,
> With hardocks, hemlock, nettles, cuckoo-flow'rs,
> Darnel and all the idle weeds that grow
> In our sustaining corn . . .
>
> (IV. iv. 3)

whose first words are 'I am the King himself', who jests and preaches (IV. vi. 181), who is filled with a conviction that he is soon to be killed ('I will die bravely, like a smug bridegroom', IV. vi. 200; 'If you have poison for me, I will drink it', IV. vii. 72), who can say: 'Nay, an you get it, you shall get it by running', and run away dressed in his flowers and pursued by the attendants;—this figure is easily recognizable. He is a Jack-a-Green, at once hero and victim of a popular ceremony. For a moment, he is a hunted man literally, as he is in spirit throughout the play. Nor is such a level of interest in any way out of place for Lear. There is much of the quality of folk thinking or acting, of the folk-tale, about his whole career. This shows in the stylized opening scene, in the formality and symmetry of his break with the three sisters, in his mock court in the outhouse and in this Jack-a-Green spectacle, right through to his final entry,—which cannot but call up the legendary 'Come not between the dragon and his wrath' of the opening tableau, and in which Lear and Cordelia must appear not as king and princess, but, beyond normal life, as emblems of the extremes of what is possible in life.

Over the four plays which have been discussed so far there seems by now to emerge, with increasing clarity, a repeated and recognizable pattern. In *Lear* it is surely inescapable. Despite the rich detail and realism of this play, the action and the staging are stylized largely throughout. The protagonist (followed, less fully but in some ways more plainly, by Gloucester) pursues a well-marked rôle. He is the man who begins as centre of his whole world, but who is progressively set, both by the other characters and by himself, apart from it and against it. 'Against' means above, in solitary defiance, and below, in an ordeal of protracted suffering which takes on the quality of a hunt. His response to this may indeed be a growing awareness and comprehension of where he stands; but if this makes the onward movement of the action profounder and more impressive, it in no way retards or re-directs it; and its end is a death which, though realistically the outcome of the human situation of the play, has at the same time the quality of stylized and ritual execution. All is foreseen, nothing can be delayed or hastened or mitigated. We are led, in fact, to envisage a new metaphor for the status of the tragic rôle in these plays; to see running through the work, besides its other interests, its detailed representation of life, its flow of ideas, its sense of good and evil, something which might be called the vertebrate structure of its intrinsic design; the developing line, unabridged, of a human sacrifice.

VI

'ANTONY AND CLEOPATRA'

THOSE WHO BELIEVE, like Mr Bithell, that 'in *Antony and Cleopatra*, Shakespeare returns to the old problem: what are the positive bases of the good life? He finds them in the affections, and in the affections as rooted deep in the sensual nature'; or like Professor Wilson Knight, that 'to understand the play aright we must be prepared to see . . . Cleopatra as love herself',[41] will think it perverse to begin a discussion of this play by quoting Shakespeare's Sonnet 129:

> The expense of spirit in a waste of shame
> Is lust in action; and till action, lust
> Is perjur'd, murd'rous, bloody, full of blame,
> Savage, extreme, rude, cruel, not to trust;
> Enjoyed no sooner but despised straight;
> Past reason hunted, and, no sooner had,
> Past reason hated, as a swallowed bait,
> On purpose laid to make the taker mad—
> Mad in pursuit, and in possession so;
> Had, having, and in quest to have, extreme;
> A bliss in proof, and prov'd, a very woe;
> Before, a joy propos'd; behind, a dream.
>> All this the world well knows; yet none knows well
>> To shun the heaven that leads men to this hell.

Yet however much it may be thought perverse to quote a sonnet on lust in the context of these lovers, it cannot be denied that at the very outset of the play Shakespeare puts before his

99

audience, as emphatically as he can, the issue of whether the spectacle before them is one of love or of lust. Philo, in his first speech, says that Antony's heart

> is become the bellows and the fan
> To cool a gipsy's *lust*.

The main characters enter, and Cleopatra's first words are: 'If it be *love indeed*, tell me how much.'

Whether Antony and Cleopatra lust, or love, or something of both, is probably a matter on which complete agreement cannot be expected. Men use these words as they are guided not only by their sense of value, but also by their experience of life; both of these are liable to much variation, and the critic may find that opportunities for augmenting the second are, in his case, slight, past or unwelcome. Sonnet 129 helps the reader of *Antony and Cleopatra* for two reasons. First it shows Shakespeare speaking of the experience of lust in a very remarkable way. Ferocious as is his condemnation of it in the earlier lines of the poem, and sorrowful as is his portrait of what follows after it is sated, for all that he calls it nothing less than 'a *bliss* in proof'. The last line is more emphatic still. Whether it refers to what precedes lust, or to the actual satisfying of lust, or to both at once, it is still nothing short of a 'heaven'. It is still to be described by no less a word than that which Cleopatra employs at the very climax of the play:

> . . . that kiss
> Which is my Heaven to have.
>   (V. ii. 300)

It is clear that 'lust', in this sonnet, means something quite different from what is occasionally termed 'cocktail sex'.

Most critics have tried (or perhaps 'struggled' is the word) to express how the relation between Antony and Cleopatra cannot be seen simply. Mr Traversi, who said that from one point of view the play was Shakespeare's supreme expression of 'love as *value*', also said that to see it as depicting a 'senseless surrender to passion' was defensible. Professor L. C. Knights refers to an 'absolute value' in the sense of heightened life and energy infused by Shakespeare into the love story, but also suggests that the energy is in Antony's own case, merely 'galvanized', and that 'the sense of potentiality in life's untutored energies' is discarded or condemned. (Whether these contradictory assertions are adequately reconciled in his description is a question which need not be pursued.) Professor Danby, starting as it were from the opposite end, writes: '*Antony and Cleopatra* is an account of things in terms of the World and the Flesh, Rome and Egypt, the two great contraries that maintain and destroy each other, considered apart from any third sphere that might stand over against them.'[42] But for Professor Danby, it transpires, the Flesh is more than some might think: it 'has its glory and passion, its witchery. Love in *Antony and Cleopatra* is both these.'

If readers find, rightly, that there is something both vague and strained about all these accounts, perhaps that is because a remarkable fact about the bond between the lovers has been consistently overlooked. Whether the bond in question is love, or passion, or both, it is neither of these which the lovers themselves mainly bring to light when they speak of each other or of what is between them. It is a certain third thing, which will prove to operate in association with these, although in essence it remains quite distinct from them.

This 'third thing' transpires from the very start. Cleopatra's first words, admittedly, were 'if it be love indeed, tell me how much'. But insofar as Antony does tell her, it is a very particular kind of 'how much' that he stresses:

> The *nobleness* of life
> Is to do thus [embracing], when such a mutual pair
> And such a twain can do 't, in which *I bind*
> *On pain of punishment, the world to weet*
> We stand up *peerless*.
>
> (I. i. 36)

Antony does not always talk so ('I' th' East my *pleasure* lies'); but this is the attitude which re-emerges at Cleopatra's death. His pointed 'I come, my queen' leads into a vision of their reunion after death; yet surely, for those who weigh it, this vision is a remarkable one:

> Where souls do couch on flowers, we'll hand in hand,
> And *with our spritely port make the ghosts gaze*.
> Dido and her Aeneas shall want troops
> And *all the haunt be ours*.
>
> (IV. xiv. 51)

The peerless pair are not re-united in the intimacy of their love for each other, but are to be the cynosure of the world to come, as they have been of this one. Antony immediately goes on to see in Cleopatra herself exactly what he had seen in his love with her

> I, that with my sword
> Quarter'd the world, and o'er green Neptune's back
> With ships made cities, condemn myself to lack
> The courage of a woman; less *noble* mind
> That she which by her death our Caesar tells
> 'I am conqueror of myself'.
>
> (IV. xiv. 57)

This sense of having the rôle of greatness to live up to, runs throughout the play. It shows at Antony's meeting with Octavius and Lepidus (see the passage quoted on p. 110), it shows in his attitude to Octavia:

> Gentle Octavia,
> Let your best love draw to that point which seeks
> Best to preserve it. If I lose mine *honour*
> I lose myself; better I were not yours
> Than yours so branchless.
>
> (III. iv. 20)

It shows in his magnanimity to the renegade Enobarbus. It is sustained (for it is, one must remember, an outward greatness, the bounteous lordliness of a colossus of public life, one who dominates the stage of history) in his feasting, his generosity, his valour and spiritedness in the last campaign against Caesar; and it is confirmed in the words of the soothsayer:

> Thy daemon, that thy spirit which keeps thee, is
> Noble, courageous, high, unmatchable. . . .
>
> (II. iii. 20)

That Antony's greatness is subject to moods of indulgence, irresponsibility and depression, and that it is far from anything which easily wins the name of greatness without reserve, is not to the point. But it is very much to the point to notice how, at an early stage in the play, it is a greatness which is one with his incomparable *physical* resilience:

> at thy heel
> Did famine follow; whom thou fought'st against,
> Though daintily brought up, with patience more
> Than savages could suffer. Thou didst drink
> The stale of horses and the gilded puddle
> Which beasts would cough at . . .
>   . . . And all this—
> It wounds thine *honour* that I speak it now—
> Was borne so like a soldier that thy cheek
> So much as lanked not.
>   (I. iv. 58)

Before this, Antony has given to the younger Pompey just such praise as he merits himself:

> who, high in name and power,
> Higher than both in *blood and life*, stands up
> For the main soldier.
>   (I. ii. 183)

Yet if Antony, at the moment of disaster and crisis, dwells less on love than on his and his queen's nobility—so does she. It is easy to allow our own familiar ideas to play too freely in our minds, and make us see Cleopatra's delight in Antony's greatness as going merely with a woman's private affection and devotion towards her mate; but when she says:

> His face was as the heav'ns . . .
> His legs bestrid the ocean; his rear'd arm
> Crested the world. His voice was propertied
> As all the tuned spheres. . . .
>   (V. ii. 79)

Dolabella, at once paying her what he sees as the acceptable compliment, guides us to how she glories in Antony's glory as counterpart to her own:

> Your loss is, *as yourself*, *great*; and you bear it
> As *answering* to the weight.
>   (V. ii. 101)

What Cleopatra sees as calling her to commit suicide is not her love and her loss; but nobility:

> Good sirs, take heart.
> We'll bury him; and then, what's *brave*, what's *noble*,
> Let's do it after the high Roman fashion,
> And *make earth proud to take us*.
>   (IV. xv. 85)

103

When she comes to die ('most *noble* Empress', Dolabella has just called her), it is '*Noble* Charmian' who means to die with her. 'What poor an instrument / May do a *noble* deed' she says when the asps are brought in (V. ii. 235); and 'Methinks I hear / Antony call. I see him rouse himself / To praise my *noble* act' she goes on. Yet is this not to imagine a lovers' reunion of a very distinctive kind? The distinctiveness is confirmed a moment later when, seeing Iras dying before her, she imagines her arriving first in the Elysian fields, and receiving from Antony 'that kiss / Which is my heaven to have'. It is clear that Antony would not kiss Iras as if she were the woman he loved: he would kiss her as a public act of recognition and high praise. Plainest of all, perhaps, is what follows the words: 'Husband, I come':

> Now to that name my *courage* prove my title
> (V. ii. 286)

The Eastern star is a fit bride for the triple pillar of the world. Her title to the honour, though, is not the completeness of her love: it is her own honour—her courage, greatness of spirit, nobility, stressed once again in the words which follow: 'I am fire and air; my other elements / I give to *baser* life.'

This antithesis between noble and base is a constant one:

> Since Cleopatra died
> I have lived in such dishonour that the gods
> Detest my baseness . . .

is Antony's expression of it (IX. xiv. 55). Cleopatra's is her 'This proves me base' (V. ii. 298) when she thinks that Iras will be first to meet Antony. To be able only to say in general terms that the love of these lovers is less than love in the fullest, or passion in the merest sense, was to say little. But here is the third term upon which Shakespeare depends to qualify the other two: that third quality of mind or emotion which exalts passion, or renders love less than itself, in a definite and distinctive way. Both the lovers find, in their love, the manifestation and continuance of their own greatness, their glory as people made on a larger and grander scale than average life. This is the kind of nobility which it has (one genuinely noble, in its way, though it has nothing of the more inward nobility of Kent or Hermione); and this is what gives it its quality of dramatized exaltation, its eloquence, its superb if also savage egotism. There is more to recognize. The love of Antony and Cleopatra is not related to their greatness as its mere effect. It is not only effect, it is also cause: it is the source of their greatness. As other lines of life are closed to them, the lovers find more and more, each in the other, an incomparable model of nobility and spirit, one which it is their over-riding thought to emulate.

Yet if Antony and Cleopatra mutually inspire each other with a spectacle of greatness, the play could not be more different than it is from, say, *Bérénice*: there is nothing remote or self-denying in their exaltation. This is because, throughout the play, Shakespeare sees the greatness of both as one with their intense and exuberant physical energy; and it seems to be part of his sense of the whole situation, that exuberance of this order actually issues, in its turn, from sexuality itself in the full tide of its fulfilment. Cleopatra's vitality—'Age cannot wither her, nor custom stale / Her infinite variety' (II. iii. 239)—is a match for Antony's as hardened campaigner; and it is a vitality that inevitably takes the form of an irresistible sexual fascination and life:

> I saw her once
> Hop forty paces through the public street;
> And having lost her breath, she spoke, and panted,
> That she did make defect perfection,
> And, *breathless, pow'r breathed forth.*
>
> (II. iii. 232)

Whatever she does, her spirits and energy turn always one way; whether it is hanging a dead fish on Antony's rod as he fishes, out-drinking him, dressing him in her own clothes as he lies in drunken sleep, or roystering in disguise with him at night. What is more, this is exactly how he sees her. Planning this night-time prank, Antony makes it plain that for him, it is Cleopatra's vitality that makes her sexually irresistible; and that it does so with a nuance that leaves her an object of wondering admiration. The sequence, 'Every passion . . . fair . . . admir'd', in the following lines (they come in the opening moments of the play, and lay down how we are to see the rest of it) set this beyond doubt:

> . . . queen . . .
> Whom everything becomes—to chide, to laugh,
> To weep; whose every passion fully strives
> To make itself in thee fair and admired.
> No messenger but thine, and all alone
> Tonight we'll wander through the streets. . . .
>
> (I. i. 48)

On the other hand, Cleopatra's image of Antony is of one whose inexhaustible vitality is physical and sexual through and through:

> For his bounty,
> There was no winter in 't; an autumn 'twas
> That grew the more by reaping. His delights
> Were dolphin-like: they showed his back above
> The element they lived in.[43]
>
> (V. ii. 86)

The third term, which explains exactly how Antony and Cleopatra do more than lust, if they do less than love, is thus their glory. Each finds in the other, and sustains in himself, a greatness which is inseparable from an incomparable physical energy; and in each, and in each's image of the other, this physical energy is an exuberant embodiment of their attraction as lovers. Nobility is a modulation of vitality, and that of sexuality. With beautiful completeness and detail (and, some will find, with a rewarding knowledge of life) Shakespeare has drawn together, as extreme links of one continuous chain

> O, see, my women,
> The crown o' th' earth doth melt. My lord!
> O, wither'd is the garland of the war . . .
>
> (IV. xv. 62)

and

> the bellows and the fan
> To cool a gipsy's lust.
>
> (I. i. 9)

The highest and lowest, the most exalted and the base, in the end were one.

At something like this point many discussions of this play, as of others, cease; their authors supposing, presumably, that the substance of the work has been dealt with. What has been dealt with so far, however, is the mere basic recipe for a situation, or merely those potential linkages and associations in human response, emotion and conduct which the work brings into play (its 'values', some would say):—but not the play that it makes with them through its unfolding action: what *transpires*, we could say, not what is *transacted*. In this latter respect *Antony and Cleopatra* is especially interesting. It arrives at a very remarkable kind of resolution—one which it is a *tour de force* on Shakespeare's part to achieve—and it does so through a rhythm of local progression which (though some have found it loose or confusing) is profoundly right for its idea and structure as a whole.

Once again, a clue may perhaps be found in Sonnet 129. This sonnet reminds us that lust, and (let us pass over experience in silence) innumerable passages in Elizabethan literature remind us that love, is a constant and vehement oscillation, an unbroken to-and-fro between positive and negative, mood and mood. So is *Antony and Cleopatra*. So, to a certain extent, is every narrative; but to notice this in *Antony and Cleopatra* is not to place an arbitrary stress, in this one case, on what could be stressed in every case. This oscillation governs the very substance of the play. 'Give me some music . . . Let it alone! Let's to billiards . . . I'll none now. Give me mine angle—we'll to the river' (II. v. 1–10) says Cleopatra while Antony is away. The messenger enters, and even before he delivers his message, she calls him a villain, gives him gold, then threatens to melt it and pour it down his throat. When she hears his news, she drives him away, calls him back, dismisses him, calls him again, dismisses him again, then sends after him to hear more. Her final thought is of Antony, and is in just the same vein: 'Let him for ever go—let him not, Charmian' (II. v. 115). She is as inconstant when Antony is at hand as when he is not: 'If you find him sad / Say I am dancing; if in mirth, report / That I am sudden sick . . .' (I. iii. 3).

Antony is the same, both as she describes him when he says, 'He was disposed to mirth; but on the sudden / A Roman thought hath struck him' (I. ii. 79); and, more substantially, in whole contrasting episodes: for example when, infatuated with Cleopatra's physical presence (I. i), he refuses to hear the ambassadors from Rome, in contrast with the later episode where he searchingly questions the same messenger, and concludes: 'I must from this enchanting queen break off' (I. ii. 125). A line earlier he confirms the point: 'The present pleasure, / By revolution low'ring, does become / The opposite of itself.' Act II scene iii epitomizes the contrast. It opens with Antony bidding goodnight to Octavia just after his betrothal to her, and the appearance, anyhow, of sincerity is decisive:

> My Octavia,
> Read not my blemishes in the world's report.
> I have not kept my square; but that to come
> Shall all be done by th' rule.
>
> (II. iii. 4)

The soothsayer enters; his warning to Antony merely echoes a truth already in the hearer's mind; and within twenty lines:

> I will to Egypt;
> And though I make this marriage for my peace,
> 'I' th' East my pleasure lies.

The other side of Antony's nature is awake.

Later in the play, Antony reverts once more:

> Ha!
> Have I my pillow left unpress'd in Rome,
> Forborne the getting of a lawful race,
> And by a gem of women, to be abus'd
> By one that looks on feeders?
>
> (III. xiii. 105)

This is what Antony says to Cleopatra when he finds her with Thyreus. In the closing scenes 'Antony / Is valiant and dejected' says Scarus (IV. xii. 6); and in the last stages of the campaign, almost unbalanced oscillation between shrewdness and folly, hopefulness and despair, love and hate, need no illustration. This constant oscillation, finally, is also symbolized in the river of Egypt itself:

Antony: . . . The higher Nilus swells
   The more it promises; as it ebbs, the seedsman
   Upon the slime and ooze scatters his grain,
   And shortly comes to harvest
            (II. vii. 20)

and gives substance to some of the most memorable images in
the play:

     This common body,
  Like to a vagabond flag upon the stream,
  Goes to and back, lackeying the varying tide,
  To rot itself with motion.

       (I. iv. 44)

  Her tongue will not obey her heart, nor can
  Her heart inform her tongue—the swan's down feather,
  That stands upon the swell at the full of tide,
  And neither way inclines.
        (III. ii. 48)

—this kind of stability is really the quintessence of vacillation.

The world of politics in this play is a world of flux as well.
That this is true of the constant to-and-fro between Rome and
Egypt, the stages where Antony plays as general and as lover,
needs no confirmation; in its wide and hurried movement
from place to place, *Antony and Cleopatra* probably stands by
itself among all Shakespeare's works. The same movement
shows in the fortunes of war, and of the diplomacy that precedes the war. Antony's position is weakening all the time; yet
it does so not through steady decline, but through a constant
alternation of failure and comparative success. More intimately,
in a sense, there is a constant oscillation in the balance of moral
evaluation. All the time, we are invited to think now better
and now worse of the scene before us; this is equally true of
public life and of private. At their first meeting (at II. ii. 27;
the passage requires study in full) Caesar and Antony are dis-
trustful of each other and careful not to lose face, but it would
be crude to accept Enobarbus's sceptical comment without
having in mind that the whole scene is a judgement, in its
turn, upon the comment. His

. . . if you borrow one another's love for the instant, you may, when
you hear no more words of Pompey, return it again . . .

is something that Maecenas has already set in a more sympathetic light:

> If it might please you to enforce no further
> The griefs between you—to forget them quite
> Were to remember that the present need
> Speaks to atone you.
>
> (II. ii. 103)

When Antony reproves Enobarbus with: 'Thou art a soldier only. Speak no more' (II. ii. 112), he is not simply excluding an honest soldier from a dishonest manoeuvre. The honesty is a kind of impercipience, the manoeuvring honest within its limits. One is likely to be told that this is naïve; but perhaps the naïveté comes in being confident of that. In fact Antony is held back by a sense of his own glory, Caesar by a sense of what is feasible; yet both speak with a note of sincerity against which Enobarbus's words have only limited weight:

> *Antony:*   As nearly as I may,
> I'll play the penitent to you; but mine honesty
> Shall not make poor my greatness . . .
> For which myself, the ignorant motive, do
> So far ask pardon as befits mine honour
> To stoop in such a case.
>
> (II. ii. 95)
>
> *Caesar:*   It cannot be
> We shall remain in friendship, our conditions
> So diff'ring in their acts. Yet if I knew
> What hoop should hold us stanch, from edge to edge
> O' th' world, I would pursue it.
>
> (II. ii. 116)

Similarly with the marriage of Antony to Octavia. Mr Traversi's reiterated 'shameful proceeding', 'supremely cynical suggestion', 'most dishonorable project', 'cynical transaction' [44] in this connection suggest a distaste against which lucidity fights a losing battle. A marriage to cement an alliance need have nothing cynical, shameful or dishonourable about it; and the play gives no reason whatever to suppose that the 'helpless sister Octavia' either was helpless in respect of her devoted brother (Shakespeare seems to follow Plutarch here),[45] or would have wished to help herself in any way other than by furthering his wishes. Attitudes like this may have become obsolete, but they are neither incomprehensible nor unattractive.

Menas: Then is Caesar and he [Antony] for ever knit together.
Enobarbus: If I were bound to divine of this unity, I would not prophesy so.
Menas: I think the policy of that purpose made more in the marriage than the love of the parties.
Enobarbus: I think so too. But you shall find the band that seems to tie their friendship together will be the very strangler of their amity.

(II. vi. 111)

There is nothing cynical in this, and if there is something un-realistic, it is balanced by what Caesar says later: instead of Enobarbus's dismissal, we have genuine awareness of a danger, envisaged openly and humanely:

> Most noble Antony,
> Let not the piece of virtue which is set
> Betwixt us as the cement of our love
> To keep it builded be the ram to batter
> The fortress of it; for better might we
> Have loved without this mean, if on both parts
> This be not cherished.
> (III. ii. 27)

Plutarch's comment again has its relevance: 'everybody con-curred in promoting this new alliance, fully expecting that . . . all would be kept in the safe and happy course of friendship.' Later on in Plutarch's account, Octavia calls herself 'the most fortunate woman on earth . . . wife and sister of the two great commanders'. These attitudes are nearer to Shakespeare's by far than those of today.

The alternations of the play continue. Caesar and Antony, at their leave-taking, plainly seem sincere in their wish for amity and affection for Octavia; but in the whispered conversation of Enobarbus and Agrippa which follows, we are at once re-minded to watch those in the game for power with an eye for their guile. Act III scene iv, and Act III scene vi, an exactly matched pair of scenes, bring out both the justice, and the petulant over-touchiness, of each commander's sense that he has been wronged by the other. Caesar's speeches at the death of Antony (V. ii. 35) and Cleopatra (V. ii. 350) cannot be cynically taken; both unmistakably justify Agrippa's 'Caesar is touched'. Yet in each, the speaker's sense of his own position and dignity is delicately but inescapably sustained.

That the fluctuations of the war are fluctuations within an over-riding direction needs no argument. But this is the medium of, and subordinate to, the play's central concern. The panorama of the Civil War, of Roman politics, is the mere occasion and reflection of the developing ordeal of Antony and Cleopatra. In this matter, Shakespeare is once again following Plutarch, who begins his summing-up of the career of Antony by saying that he was among 'great examples of the vicissitudes of Fortune'; by which Plutarch did not mean the constant and directionless fluctuations of life, but the great reversals which bring men from the summit of fortune to its nadir.

Shakespeare is writing with just such an event in mind; and he gives it the emphasis which has been observed in the earlier tragedies. Here, as before, the protagonists begin not merely at the height of Fortune, but as the cynosure and exemplar of all. Antony is 'the triple pillar of the world' (I. i. 12), and

> The demi-Atlas of this earth, the arm
> And burgonet of men.
>
> (I. v. 23)

Enobarbus's account of Cleopatra on the barge culminates in the idea that she was in the most literal sense the object of everyone's gaze, the ceremonial figure in the centre of the stage. But so (except for her) was Antony:

> The city cast
> Her people out upon her; *and Antony*
> *Enthron'd i' th' market-place*, did sit alone
> Whistling to th' air; which, but for vacancy,
> Had gone to gaze on Cleopatra too,
> And made a gap in nature.
>
> (II. iii. 217)

Yet at once, the play instructs its audience to watch for the beginning of a change. 'You have seen and prov'd a fairer former fortune / Than that which is to approach', says the soothsayer to Charmian (I. ii. 32); 'Ten thousand harms, more than the ills I know, / My idleness doth hatch' (I. ii. 126) is

Antony's statement of it (I. ii. 126); or again 'Much is breeding / Which, like the courser's hair, hath yet but life / And not a serpent's poison.' (I. ii. 186.) Accept these as guides, and one cannot but begin to trace a now familiar kind of movement. Despite all differences of situation or character, the resemblance is plain, at a radical level, with the careers of Hamlet, Othello, Macbeth and Lear.

Antony and Cleopatra both estrange themselves from the environment they grandiosely dominate. Antony's curse on the world of his public life:

> Let Rome in Tiber melt, and the wide arch
> Of the rang'd empire fall! Here is my space . . . .
> (I. i. 33)

is something which Cleopatra exactly parallels for hers. (The lines have a special prominence at the end of Act I.)

> Get me ink and paper.
> He shall have every day a several greeting,
> Or I'll *unpeople Egypt*.

Cleopatra in her career of malediction pursues a course reminiscent of Lear: moving from the local to the general, from country to cosmos, from 'Sink Rome, and their tongues rot / That speak against us!' (III. vii. 15) to 'O sun, Burn the great sphere thou mov'st in! Darkling stand / The varying shore o' th' world' (IV. xv. 9). Antony confirms his status as a gigantic outlaw among mankind by his treatment of Thyreus. The ill-treatment of a messenger is as much a conventionalized act of decisive self-condemnation as Lear's division of the kingdom; and Antony himself, while his position is still relatively undamaged (or at least, still in question or in the balance) reminds the audience of the status of what later on he is to do:

Antony: Well, what worst?
Messenger: The nature of bad news infects the teller.
Antony: When it concerns the fool or coward. On!
             Things that are past are done with me. 'Tis thus:
             Who tells me true, though in his tale lie death,
             I hear him as he flattered. . . .
             Speak to me home; mince not the general tongue.
                          (I. ii. 91)

This messenger is one of Antony's servants while Thyreus is one of Caesar's, but that makes the parallel only the more telling; and Cleopatra's ill-treatment of the messenger bringing news of Antony's marriage is plainly part of the same carefully-pointed sequence of events.

Macbeth cuts himself off from Duncan and Banquo: the Doctor, and those who flee to the English army, cut themselves off from him. Lear rejects Cordelia and Kent, and receives the like at the hands of Regan and Goneril. To begin with, Antony is isolated and alienated of his own choice. He dismisses the concerns of the Empire, and when we see him (III. iv) sending away Octavia, we know his ulterior motive for doing so. But things do not end as they began. The words of Canidius make clear what is happening: 'To Caesar will I render / My legions and my horse; six kings already / Show me the way of yielding' (III. x. 33); and the movement is elevated to the plane of the symbolic:

Second Soldier: Hark!
Third Soldier:　　　　Music i' th' air.
Fourth Soldier:　　　　　　　　Under the earth.
Third Soldier: It signs well, does it not?
Fourth Soldier:　　　　　　　No.
Third Soldier:　　　　　　　　　　Peace, I say!
　　　　　What should this mean?
Second Soldier: 'Tis the god Hercules, whom Antony lov'd,
　　　　　Now leaves him.
　　　　　　　　　　　(IV. iii. 13)

Hercules' example is followed by the man whom Antony most loved, Enobarbus (IV. v); and in a sense by Eros, who refuses (though out of devotion) to do Antony the last service of killing him. Until the death of Antony, no one can significantly desert Cleopatra; but as soon as she is left unsupported, she is first deceived by Proculeius, the one man whom Antony advised her to trust (V. ii. 35; cf. IV. xv. 48), and then by Seleucus her eunuch (V. ii. 144).

Cleopatra, driven to the refuge of her monument and then snared in it, makes a spectacle a little like that of a creature being hunted; and the same idea is clearly worked into the text as an image of the last days of Antony. The word 'hunted' is in fact used fairly early on:

> Caesar must think
> When one so great begins to rage, he's *hunted*
> *Even to falling. Give him no breath* but now
> Make boot of his distraction.
>
> (IV. i. 6)

Othello driven to his utmost sea-mark, or Macbeth or Gloucester tied like a bear to the stake, have their parallel in his own predicament:

> Unarm, Eros; the long day's task is done,
> And we must sleep . . . So it must be, for now
> All length is torture. Since the torch is out.
> Lie down, and stray no further.
>
> (IV. xiv. 35)

The ordeal of Antony is a hunt, and ends as a hunt ends.

Charmian, at one point in the play, invites the audience to see Antony's career just as Plutarch did, as a great example of the vicissitude of Fortune:

> The soul and body rive not more in parting
> Than *greatness going off.*
>
> (IV. xiii. 5)

But if Antony may justly say, through the long-drawn-out 'agony' (in the strict sense), 'the shirt of Nessus is upon me' (IV. xii. 43), there is more to this ordeal than this brings out. Or rather, there is a response in him to that ordeal, for which again the clue is in Plutarch: 'It was his character in calamities to be better than at any other time. Antony in misfortune was most nearly a virtuous man.' Caesar's tribute to how Antony rose above misfortune in his early campaigns has already been quoted (p. 103). This heightened nobility as misfortune gathers about him is plain, and sometimes febrilely over-plain, in his final moments of valour:

> I would they'd fight i' th' fire or i' th' air;
> We'd fight there too.
>
> (IV. x. 3)

But it would be wholly false to see this side of Antony, in the closing phase of the drama, as self-discrediting. There is nothing self-discrediting in his forgiveness and generosity for Enobarbus:

> Go, Eros, send his treasure after; do it;
> Detain no jot, I charge thee. Write to him—
> I will subscribe—gentle adieus and greetings;
> Say that I wish he never more find cause
> To change a master. O, my fortunes have
> Corrupted honest men. Dispatch. Enobarbus!
>
> (IV. v. 12)

Moreover a new note is heard. Here Antony is speaking with the simplicity and directness not of a public figure, but of a man whose inner life has been touched; and later, his dying words, in spite of what they say, are simple and sincere:

> The miserable change now at my end
> Lament nor sorrow at; but please your thoughts
> In feeding them with those my former fortunes
> Wherein I liv'd the greatest prince o' th' world,
> The noblest; and do now not basely die,
> Not cowardly put off my helmet to
> My countryman—a Roman by a Roman
> Valiantly vanquish'd. Now my spirit is going
> I can no more.[46]
>
> (IV. xv. 51)

This is not empty boasting, partly because it is the simple truth that Antony was the greatest and noblest prince in the world, but chiefly because of the tone; in which, more than in his challenging Caesar to single combat (though that too plays its clearly qualified part), we should see something of how Antony was at his best in calamity. It does so, one might say, through indicating that a part of that 'best' was for him to take on a 'baseness' more significantly the opposite of his valour, his greatness, than the baseness which he fears (and by fits succumbs to). Just as in the retreat from Modena the greatness of the general showed in his readiness to drink filth and eat the bark of trees, so now, along with Antony's exaltation in the face of disaster, there begins to come into the play a new sense of his basic and essential humanity.

> I here importune death awhile, until
> Of many thousand kisses *the poor last*
> I lay upon thy lips.
>
> (IV. xv. 19)

This is a 'nobleness of life' which hints at a new inwardness and depth; in which, perhaps, many readers today will see, for the first time in Antony, something which is of the spirit not the *persona*, and which they are really willing to call nobility.

'Begins to come into the play', and begins only, however. Shakespeare's sense of what such a nature as Antony's, or Cleopatra's, will do when stretched to breaking-point is complex and complete, but he husbands his resources. He sees both the central characters as impelled into conduct which is sometimes exalted and sometimes abject (Antony's railing at the queen, her several attempts to make terms with Caesar, and finally her subterfuge for keeping back her treasure); and he also sees both as partially divested of the trappings of greatness, because their essential being as humans, their innermost condition of 'unaccommodated man', begins in calamity to transpire. But this final turn of the situation he merely hints at with Antony, because he saves its full development for Cleopatra.

Cleopatra's death-scene is the anti-type of Enobarbus's picture of her in all her splendour:

> Now, Charmian!
> Show me, my woman, like a queen. Go fetch
> My best attires. *I am again for Cydnus*
> To meet Mark Antony. . . .
> Give me my robe, put on my crown; I have
> Immortal longings in me. . . .
>
> (V. ii. 226, 278)

The exaltation of the scene, as a moment of supreme greatness, is also made plain in words which gain part of their force from their echo of Antony (the passage was quoted on p. 115):

> I am fire and air; my other elements
> I give to baser life.
>
> (V. ii. 287)

But if it is such a moment, the supreme greatness is also to do the one thing left to do in a hopeless, helpless case. 'Bravest at the last', Caesar says; but it is bravery with a new quality, less 'brave' in the Elizabethan sense, more poignant. The quite

new note of a private and personal distress, when Antony calls
her down from the monument:

> I dare not, dear.
> Dear my lord, pardon! *I dare not,*
> *Lest I be taken . . .*
> (IV. xv. 21)

leads into her new picture of herself after she has swooned. The
great queen begins to be one with women at the other extreme
of humanity:

> No more but e'en a woman, and commanded
> By such poor passion as the maid that milks
> And does the meanest chores.
> (IV. xv. 73)

This new idea of Cleopatra is sustained, immediately before her
death, in the scene of her homely conversation with the 'simple
countryman' who brings the asps; and (fused with its antithesis)
continues in Charmian's

> Now boast thee, death, in thy possession lies
> A *lass* unparalleled.
> (V. ii. 313)

Shakespeare's picture of Cleopatra as 'no more but e'en a
woman' was also prepared for in other ways. It seems likely
that the celebrated lines:

> Do you not see my baby at my breast
> That sucks the nurse asleep?
> (V. ii. 307)

resume the image which Cleopatra has already drawn when
she envisaged her death at the beginning of the scene: and offers
us reason, perhaps, for accepting the well-known emendation:

> it is great
> To do that thing that ends all other deeds,
> Which shackles accidents and bolts up change,
> Which sleeps, and never palates more the *dug*,
> The beggar's *nurse*, and Caesar's.
> (V. ii. 4)

Death is a nurse, and at the end of the day she does not feed the
child any longer, because she falls asleep.

'The beggar's nurse and Caesar's.' A moment later, Cleopatra
uses the antithesis again: 'If your master / Would have a queen
his beggar . . .' (V. ii. 15). 'Beggar' goes with another strand in
the converging pattern of suggestion. As the play closes, the
Cleopatra who chats with the countryman and dresses in her
finery, becomes (one might put it) a gipsy in a new sense, and
with a deeper meaning. The idea of dying an outcast's death
has already been set in the audience's mind through Enobarbus's resolution to

> go seek
> Some ditch wherein to die; the foul'st best fits
> My latter part of life.
>
> (IV. vi. 37)

and also through Cleopatra's curse upon herself, her children,
and her people if it is true that she is cold-hearted:

> Ah, dear, if it be so
> From my cold heart let heaven engender hail. . . .
> Till by degrees the memory of my womb
> Together with my brave Egyptians all,
> By the discandying of this pelleted storm,
> Lie graveless, till the flies and gnats of Nile
> Have buried them for prey.
>
> (III. xiii. 158)

(which Mr Traversi, in one of his more remarkable *trouvailles*,
calls 'the most complete example of Cleopatra's conversion of
slime into fertility'). At the moment of Cleopatra's death, these
ideas re-appear. They do so, because only just behind the stage
spectacle of the queen of Egypt in all her glory, is the sense of
an outcast from society—gipsy, felon, whatever it may be—
baited as the victim of the common people:

> Now, Iras, what think'st thou?
> Thou an Egyptian puppet shall be shown
> In Rome as well as I. Mechanic slaves,
> With greasy aprons, rules, and hammers, shall
> Uplift us to the view; in their thick breaths,
> Rank of gross diet, shall we be enclouded. . . .
>
> (V. ii. 206)

In this, she is merely rehearsing what Antony already described in his moment of rage with her:

> Let him take thee
> And hoist thee up to the shouting Plebeians;
>   . . . most monster-like be shown
> For poor'st diminutives, for doits, and let
> Patient Octavia plough thy visage up
> With her prepared nails.
>
>   (IV. xii. 33)

Though the appearance of Cleopatra in the moment of her death may be great and splendid, the reality comes close to that very different idea of death, drawing upon all these passages, which comes into her mind when she is first captured:

> Know, sir, that I
> Will not wait pinion'd at your master's court,
> Nor once be chastis'd by the sober eye
> Of dull Octavia. Shall they hoist me up,
> And show me to the shouting varletry
> Of censuring Rome? Rather a ditch in Egypt
> Be gentle grave unto me! Rather on Nilus' mud
> Lay me stark-naked, and let the water-flies
> Blow me into abhorring! Rather make
> My country's high Pyramides my gibbet,
> And hang me up in chains!
>
>   (V. ii. 52)

—outcast or outlaw, it is with images like these that the play surrounds Cleopatra's death in our imaginations. Caesar's closing tribute to the nobleness of both queen and servants fuses with a sense of Cleopatra's having been brought to the level of humanity at its simplest and most primitive; to the bed-rock of life. As near to an animal as a human creature can come, the victim is hunted by his own kind until, with whatever justice and whatever nobility, his life is taken. Death is no mere crowning misfortune; it is almost recognized, by pro-tagonist and pursuers alike, as the stylized act which fitly closes a stylized sequence. This sequence is beginning to seem like a recurrent *motif* in the tragedies. It is the ordeal of the great and alienated who are pursued by life until they are sacrificed.

VII

'CORIOLANUS'
'TIMON OF ATHENS'

THE PREVIOUS FIVE CHAPTERS have brought out a number
of prominent differences, in narrative or idea, between the
plays. The whole shape of *Macbeth* expresses the notion that
what disrupts the social or natural order may be destroyed in
its turn, and order restored. This is present in *King Lear* only
in what might be called a muted or negative form: there, evil
destroys itself, but that is something short of the restoration of
good. To the actions of *Othello*, and *Antony and Cleopatra*, this
notion is not really relevant. Again, there is a strong sense that
the actions of *Hamlet* and *Macbeth* work out, directly and substantially, how fortune in men's affairs can operate retributively: that is to say, how the disasters which overtake men are
significantly like those they planned for others. In *King Lear*,
one could say, the idea was present: Lear, cruel to one of his
daughters, falls victim to the cruelty of the other, Gloucester's
bastard is undutiful, and the hard-hearted sisters fall through
their infatuation for Edmund. Yet while retribution could be
said to transpire from the play, it is not transacted as one of the
substantial interests; which it is in the other two. Another
prominent difference lies in the response which the protagonists
develop to their ordeal, as it develops. Presumably there is no
need to elaborate once again how this response is more important in some cases than in others, and how, where it is
important, its nature varies from case to case.

It is in place, perhaps, to notice how (vary though they may in the different plays) the relevant ideas are those of Shakespeare's time, not of ours. Among contemporary ideas which have transpired as being especially relevant are the peculiarly intense evil of revolt in any form, the strong traditional sense of authority and subservience within the family (sister to brother and wife to husband as much as child to parent); and the sense of greatness as grandeur, of nobility as a kind of behaviour, as well as (or to a limited extent even without regard to) the inner condition which creates and imposes it. Those who admire Shakespeare, but find these ideas unattractive, may be reluctant to admit their presence, or at least their importance, in his work; but the denial cannot be sustained. The main point, however, is to notice how these ideas, recurrent though they may be in the plays, vary greatly in importance and emphasis from one play to another.

There are reasons, undoubtedly, why it might be best to give all the emphasis to the differences between play and play; for the desire to concentrate attention on Shakespeare's plays as a single developing *oeuvre* has sometimes had unfortunate results. But one thing, which seems to recur through these tragedies, is embodied in their actions as wholes, and is so substantial that it must be given attention. This recurrent feature is connected with something referred to in the first chapter of this book, the wholly distinctive prominence of the central characters; and it relates to what distinguishes the whole pattern of development embodied in their experience, their whole ordeal of action and suffering.

On the one hand, this ordeal of the protagonist moves from one extreme of the social group to the other. Nor has this meant simply, from the top of Fortune's wheel to the bottom. These tragic protagonists occupy the pinnacle of Fortune in a special way. They are not merely at the height of prosperity or greatness. They are 'the observed of all observers', the man sought by everyone, the saviour of the state, the centre of its ceremony, the central figure of the court, the senate, the battle-field, the throne in the market-place. Nor is their progress one merely of declining fortune. It is one of progressive isolation, in the course of which real deference becomes nominal, empty, and even hostile (Hamlet with Rosenkranz or Polonius, Lear with his cruel daughters, Cleopatra with her steward), or is replaced by open estrangement. Moreover, the end of this change is as distinctive as the change itself. The protagonist does not simply die, by violence or otherwise, as the last of his misfortunes. To a greater or lesser extent, his case is presented as one in which ceremonial and deference turn into a pursuit, a hunt; in the course of which there comes a point when, fleeing from disaster, he can flee no further. At this point, he turns and faces destruction; and his death is made to seem like an execution, or a sacrificial rite, or something of both.

This external process is counterpart to what might be termed a mental history undergone within the protagonist's own consciousness. The cynosure falls into a kind of *hybris*; but we should not suppose that *hybris* necessarily takes the form which it takes here. The *hybris* of Oedipus, for example, is a confidence in his power to do good excessive enough to blind him to the comparative powerlessness of all men, and to make him fail in deference where deference is due. Recurrently in his tragedies, Shakespeare seems to have been drawn to the depiction of something more far-reaching than this: a grandiose and progressive aberration in which the greatest of mankind, the pinnacle of nature's achievement, is as it were cast loose at the top end of the scale, to become alienated from and in the end an enemy of his fellows and the rest of nature. Of Hamlet and Othello, the most that can be said is that this is incipient in them, because of how they call on the powers of Hell to assist in their designs. But in *Macbeth*, calling on these powers is most emphatically given the meaning which is now at issue; and in Macbeth himself, in Lear, and in Antony and Cleopatra, one can see developing what might almost be termed a tragic liturgy of curse and defiance, a liturgy which spreads progressively wider in its reference, and settles into shape, ultimately, as justification of what overtakes the speaker. Here, too, is what creates the ambiguity of the later scenes of the plays. The action is not simply that of fortunate hero transformed into unfortunate. The transformation is of cynosure at once into a victim and a monster. If this idea is irrelevant to Hamlet, that (despite obvious distinctions, especially with Lear, which it will readily occur to the reader to draw) is the only play of which quite this may be said.

Coriolanus and *Timon of Athens* will be discussed from a point of view which is not quite that of the earlier chapters. There, the plays were considered for themselves; and the element of recurrence in the patterns of their actions was something which emerged from the discussions as merely one respect in which the plays offered interest. Almost the opposite approach will be made to the two plays which remain. No doubt they might be discussed from many points of view, and of course they offer interest of many kinds; but here they have a special value and interest. The pattern of action which has emerged from the other plays shows very clearly, indeed almost barely and baldly, in them. Whether in the last analysis this adds to their interest or detracts from it is not at present at issue. But if the time has come to move from discussions of single plays to a review of what has emerged as something running through several plays, then at this stage *Coriolanus* and *Timon* can prove particularly helpful. They make the recurrent element so clear that it becomes out of the question to argue that it is being stressed wilfully. The last chapter of the book, going forward from this point, suggests some reasons why this recurrent thread may be the foundation of a dramatic or literary experience of high importance.

It has been suggested that *Coriolanus* is at least as much a debate as a tragedy:[47] and the element of debate in it need not be denied, provided one has in mind that it is a debate concerned to sharpen the contrast between two views, or make each of two views as plausible as possible, rather than insist on a decision in favour of one or the other. Tragedy enters life at least as often because there is no right choice, as because when there is a right choice men choose wrong in preference to it; and if, on the whole, it transpires from *Coriolanus* that the tribunes are more wrong than the protagonist, or wrong in a way which invites more downright or disdainful condemnation, this is barely the matter on which the stress falls. One thing which shows how evenly the balance is kept is that Shakespeare uses the same images (or nearly so) for the mob on one hand, and the protagonist on the other. Comenius, speaking of the common people

> whose rage doth rend
> Like interrupted waters, and o'erbear
> What they are us'd to bear
>
> (III. i. 248)

is using an established metaphor for the people, that of the raging and uncontrollable river employed by Machiavelli in the celebrated chapter XXV of *Il Principe*; but earlier in the play the same speaker, saying that Coriolanus 'wax'd like a sea' (II. ii. 97), has spoken of the other side in almost the same terms. Because they are uttered in anger and as abuse, the parallels repeatedly drawn between the common people and the less noble animals (geese, mice, kites, crows by Coriolanus; cats by Volumnia) ought not to be given too solemn a meaning. They lack the resonance of similar comparisons in Lear. For all that, their quality of the grotesque bears upon an important idea in the play, that of the mob as monster:

> If he tell us of his noble deeds, we must also tell him our noble acceptance of them. Ingratitude is monstrous, and for the multitude to be ingrateful were to make a monster of the multitude; of the which we being members should bring ourselves to be monstrous members.
>
> (*Third Citizen*; II. iii. 6)

Shakespeare, of course, does not endorse the idea of mob as monster out and out. Neither is it peculiar to him: 'If there be any among those common objects of hatred I do contemn and laugh at, it is that great enemy of Reason, Virtue and Religion, the Multitude: that numerous piece of monstrosity, which, taken asunder, seem men, and the reasonable creatures of God; but, confused together, make but one great beast, and a monstrosity more prodigious than hydra.' [48]

Yet if (as Thomas Browne argues) the crowd is monstrous, so is Coriolanus its antitype. As with Lear ('Come not between the dragon and his wrath') and Macbeth, there is something of this quite early in the play; but since the monster is rather what Coriolanus becomes in the course of the action, one must first notice how clearly, both when the play opens and subsequently, he is the 'observed of all observers'. Before the play opens, we are told, 'youth with comeliness *pluck'd all gaze his way*' (I. iii. 6). He returned from his first campaign as the chief hero, 'his brows bound with oak', cynosure of the triumph. Twice, his return from the Corioli campaign is described (again, he is the oak-crowned hero of the scene), and each time the culminating point is the same:

> I have seen the dumb men throng to see him and
> The blind to hear him speak; matrons flung gloves,
> Ladies and maids their scarves and handkerchers
> Upon him as he pass'd; the nobles bended
> *As to Jove's statue,* and the commons made
> A shower and thunder with their caps and shouts
> I never saw the like.
>
> (II. ii. 252)

These words of the Messenger merely repeat Brutus's lines, perhaps for their strength and detail the most memorable in the play:

> All tongues speak of him and the bleared sights
> Are spectacled to see him. Your prattling nurse
> Into a rapture lets her baby cry
> While she chats him; the kitchen malkin pins
> Her richest lockran 'bout her reechy neck,
> Clamb'ring up walls to eye him; stalls, bulks, windows,
> Are smother'd up, leads fill'd and ridges hors'd
> With variable complexions, all agreeing
> In earnestness to see him. Seld-shown flamens
> Do press among the popular throngs and puff
> To win a vulgar station; our veil'd dames
> Commit the war of white and damask in
> Their nicely gawded cheeks to th' wanton spoil
> Of Phoebus' burning kisses. Such a pother,
> *As if that whatsoever god who leads him*
> *Were slily crept into his human powers,*
> And gave him graceful posture.
>
> (II. ii. 195)

Coriolanus enjoys another such triumph a third time at the end of the play, when he returns to Corioli (in sharp contrast to its native Aufidius) 'splitting the air with noise' (V. vi. 52). But long before that time, Coriolanus as centre of attraction has taken on a new appearance, and has come to seem god-like with a difference.

Even in the first scene, along with references to his 'greatness' and 'nobility' (ll. 174, 228), we have the words of the tribunes, of challengeable authority, but nevertheless pointing in a by now familiarly disquieting direction:

> *Brutus:* Being mov'd, he will not spare to gird the gods.
> *Sicinius:* Bemock the modest moon.
>
> (I. i. 254)

Coriolanus's image more than once recalls Macbeth, though here the emblem is one less of revolt than of dissension: 'Who's yonder / That does appear as he were flay'd?' (I. vi. 22); and '. . . from face to foot / He was a thing of blood',

> *whose every motion*
> *Was tim'd with dying cries.*
> (II. ii. 106)

If it is unnecessary to follow Professor Enright in seeing this as a suggestion that Coriolanus was like a 'mechanical juggernaut'[49] (the contemporary image, familiar from *Macbeth*, lies ready to hand, and the likelihood that Shakespeare knew what juggernauts were is slight), Coriolanus is nevertheless presented elsewhere in such inhuman terms as lay within his creator's knowledge:

When he walks, he moves like an *engine*, and the ground shrinks before his treading. He is able to pierce a corslet with his eye, talks like a knell, and his hum is a battery.

But in this image Shakespeare employs a double metaphor. What makes the ground shake as it treads, and can pierce armour with its gaze, is not a siege engine, but the monstrous beast of which Menenius has just spoken: 'This Marcius has grown from man to *dragon*' (V. iv. 13). The analogy, familiar already from *Othello* and *Lear*, comes elsewhere:

> —though I go alone,
> Like to a lonely dragon, that his fen
> Makes fear'd and talk'd of more that seen . . .
> (IV. i. 29)

says Coriolanus himself when he is being exiled. Aufidius on the march to Rome says that he 'fights dragon-like' (IV. vii. 23). The course of the play, from man into monster, is perfectly clear.

What becomes inhuman is the defiantly superhuman. The tribunes' picture of Coriolanus defiant and blasphemous comes by no means alone. 'You speak o' th' people / As if you were a god, to punish', says Brutus, when Coriolanus has become enraged at being denied entry to the market-place (III. i. 80).

The comment is not unjust, and is confirmed by Menenius's summing-up later:

> His nature is too noble for the world.
> (III. i. 255)

where 'noble' clearly refers to matchless spirit and grandiosity of conduct. 'I banish you!' is his superbly arrogant retort to the mob (III. iii. 125). On his vindictive return to Rome, the change is plainer still. The by now recognizable course is being run: the god-like man, pinnacle of Nature, is becoming a creature having no link with nature; then essentially foreign to it; and in the end, enemy to it. Three passages make these very points. The first is what Coriolanus says when his kinsfolk come to plead with him:

> I'll never
> Be such a gosling to obey instinct, but stand
> As if a man were author of himself
> And knew no other kin.
> (V. iii. 34)

Comenius is more explicit:

> he leads them like a thing
> *Made by some other deity than Nature.*
> (IV. vi. 91)

But Coriolanus himself brings out the final stage, and completes a movement which, barely hinted at with Hamlet, was made emphatic and clear for Othello, Macbeth and Lear:

> I will fight
> Against my canker'd country with the spleen
> *Of all the under fiends.*
> (IV. v. 90)

The very summit of mankind, alienated from it, in the end allies with its enemies.

Yet Coriolanus goes straight on, without the break of a single word, to display the other side of this picture, and invite us to see the monstrous and grandiose as having about it also something of the victim and the sacrifice. Again, the words are reminiscent of others of Shakespeare's protagonists, notably Macbeth and Lear:

... Of all the under fiends. But if so be
Thou dar'st not this, and that to prove more fortunes
Tho' art tir'd, then, in a word, I also am
Longer to live most weary, and present
My throat to thee and to thy ancient malice. ...

This picture, as of the weary quarry yielding itself to the
hunter, should be seen in the light of Menenius's words earlier
on to the common people:

> Do not cry havoc, where you should but *hunt*
> With modest warrant.
>
> (III. i. 275)

Yet in the main the analogy is not with hunting an animal.
Rather, it is with the pursuit and killing of a ritual victim, a
scapegoat; as the tribunes suggest in telling the people to bait
Coriolanus as they drive him out:

> *Go see him out at gates*, and *follow him*,
> As he hath follow'd you, *with all despite;*
> *Give him deserv'd vexation.*
>
> (III. iii. 139)

These lines cannot but recall Regan's 'Go thrust him out at
gates' about the blinded Gloucester; but they show how, in
Coriolanus, a physical process of expulsion from the group seems
to come as the blatant outward token of that progressive isolation from other characters which has been noticed as recurrent.
Moreover, they set Act II scene iii, when Coriolanus in his
rags supplicates for the consulship, in a sharp and special light.
Other features of the play suggest strongly that Coriolanus is a
kind of scapegoat figure, and here his status is very plainly that
of the scapegoat early in his career, when he is still an honoured
centre of attention, and yet at the same time beginning to be a
victim and a suppliant.

Twice more, in the course of the play, Coriolanus invites his
own death. Each time he envisages it as a ritual execution.

> Let them pull all about mine ears, present me
> Death on the wheel or at wild horses' heels;
> Or pile ten hills on the Tarpeian rock,
> That the precipitation might down stretch
> Below the beam of sight. ...
>
> (III. ii. 1)

This was his response to the threats of the tribunes; and immediately before his own death it is the same:

> Cut me to pieces, Volsces; men and lads,
> Stain all your edges on me.
>
> (V. vi. 112)

Needless to say, the death of Coriolanus is almost as much a *sparagmos* of the ritual victim by the whole social group as was possible on the stage:

All the People: Tear him to pieces. Do it presently.
He killed my son. My daughter. He kill'd my cousin
Marcus. He kill'd my father.
... *Conspirators:* Kill, kill, kill, kill, kill him.

So far as the spectacle on the stage is concerned, he dies at the hands of the mob, and is trampled on by Aufidius.

These details all come together to make it clear that the recurrent pattern of the plays is especially clear in *Coriolanus*. This is particularly so of the *meaning* of certain parts of the whole movement. The gradual isolation undergone by other protagonists is replaced here by the overt transformation of hero into outcast through a ceremonial act of expulsion by the group. The status of the protagonist as at once cynosure and victim or suppliant, traceable in the scene of Lear's recovery, emphasized in imagination only for Antony and Cleopatra when they are thought of as the show pieces in Caesar's triumph, is amplified repeatedly in *Coriolanus*. The protagonist appears in triumph, and also as meanly disguised and a suppliant (IV. v); and in the market-place scene, supplicating in a robe of humility for the supreme office of consul, he is something exactly between the two. Finally, in Coriolanus's death the situation is unmistakably one of the now isolated figure suffering what has the nature of a ritual killing required by society. It is death ritualized into a social event. Perhaps this makes the nature of the closing scenes in *Othello*, *Macbeth* and *Antony and Cleopatra* clearer than it was; and at the close of *Lear*, the relation between the isolated individual and the group about him is suggestively similar to this; although it is overtly brought about by circumstances, and only indirectly is it imposed by the group on the individual.

Turning from *Coriolanus* to *Timon of Athens* is perhaps the right moment to say that the problem at present is not, of course, to prove that 'just the same things' happen in one of Shakespeare's tragedies after another. If there is a movement common to them all, it is something at a radical level, something which brings together the careers of Lear and Coriolanus, although the former (like Timon) 'abjures all roofs', while the latter is banished; and the deaths of Coriolanus and Timon, although the first is massacred while the second commits suicide. With this in mind, the relevance of *Timon* becomes obvious, and since it is being discussed in the context only of the present argument, it may be discussed in brief. When the play opens, Timon is radiant with prosperity, but more than this he is the most clearly a cynosure of all Shakespeare's protagonists. The Poet, the Painter, the Jeweller and the Merchant all enter as the play opens with their offerings, paid or unpaid, for the great man. 'Look how this lord is followed!', says the Painter as the Senators come in next. The poet explains that his poem is a tribute to one who is called by Fortune to the top of her hill, and because of this is the favourite of his fellows:

> I have in this rough work shap'd out a man
> Whom this beneath world doth embrace and hug
> With amplest entertainment.
>
> (I. i. 46)

Then, as soon as the hero of the poem is called by the goddess fortune to eminence:

> All those which were his fellows but of late
> . . . on the moment
> Follow his strides, his lobbies fill with tendance,
> Rain sacrificial whisperings in his ear,
> Make sacred even his stirrup, and through him
> Drink the free air.

The words 'sacrificial', 'sacred' are full of meaning for the play; which passes rapidly through the scene of the mock banquet (at which the host is both the lord and the victim of the others) and then Timon's self-expulsion from Athens: which is as much emphasized as the enforced expulsion of Coriolanus, in that the stage spectacle of it opens Act IV:

> Let me look back upon thee. O thou wall
> That girdles in those wolves, dive in the earth
> And fence not Athens. . . .

In the closing scenes, when Timon is at the nadir of fortune, the words of Apemantus are sufficient guide: 'The middle of humanity thou never knewest, but the extremity of both ends'. As this movement continues, the alienation of Timon first from his fellows, and then from the whole of creation, is represented to begin with by how he says that he is alien to men and one with the beasts:

> Timon will to the woods, where he shall find
> Th' unkindest beast more kinder than mankind.
>
> (IV. i. 35)

('Kinder' could still mean 'corresponding to his nature'.) But this side of the play shows most clearly—and there is no need to draw attention to the parallel with other plays—in the incomparable series of maledictions which Timon pronounces in the course of Act IV. It is a series, in fact, which culminates in what is more than a malediction. First, Timon curses only mankind:

> Matrons, turn incontinent.
> Obedience fail in children! Slaves and fools,
> Pluck the grave wrinkled Senate from the bench
> And minister in their steads. To general filths
> Convert, o' th' instant, green virginity . . .
>
> (IV. i. 3)

Two scenes later, he calls on the sun to bring evil on the whole of created nature:

> O blessed breeding sun, draw from the earth
> Rotten humidity; below thy sister's orb
> Infect the air!
>
> (IV. iii. 1; cf. IV. iii. 176)

But the final horror envisaged in this extraordinary scene is that there is simply no need to curse Nature: in Timon's eyes it is accursed already:

> The sun's a thief, and with his great attraction
> Robs the vast sea; the moon's an arrant thief,
> And her pale fire she snatches from the sun;
> The sea's a thief, whose liquid surge resolves
> The moon into salt tears; the earth's a thief,
> That feeds and breeds by a composture stol'n
> From general excrement—each thing's a thief.
>
> (IV. iii. 434)

It is also clear that the play likens Timon to the sun. 'Men shut their doors against a setting sun', says Apemantus (I. ii. 139); and the idea recurs:

> You must consider, that a prodigal course
> Is like the sun's, but not like his recoverable.
>
> (III. iv. 12)

The four white horses given to Timon by the Lord Lucius have an association with the Phaeton myth. The second Lord says to Timon 'the swallows follow not summer more willingly than we your lordship' (III. vi. 29). Timon introduces the idea himself at the close; not only in saying 'Sun hide thy beams, Timon hath done his reign' (V. i. 221), but in the very act of setting his grave on the seashore, where it is swallowed up, like the sun itself, by the sea every day. In view of the fact that scapegoat rituals have so often been fertility rituals, and these, in their turn, sun rituals, there may be a temptation to see in Timon a symbol of the sun as universal fertility, and even to argue that the triumphal entry of Alcibiades at the close represents the arrival of the new 'Golden Bough' priest-king figure to replace the departed one. This lacks conviction. If the play has a ritual aspect, it is one without a particularized meaning of this kind. The analogy between Timon and the sun in no sense makes him a symbol of the sun's fertility: its contribution is that it induces us to see his fall as having the inevitability of the sun's decline; as no oddity of an individual history, but (extreme and indeed unique as it is in its degree, a point which the words of Apemantus made clear) a known and recognizable kind of thing. Once again, through the accidents of particularity, we recognize a kind of event which once begun runs its course.

Although it would be fanciful to see Timon as a ritual victim in the crude sense of seeing his career as a kind of fertility ceremony, he is clearly a victim for all that. 'It grieves me to see so many *dip their meat in one man's blood*', says Apemantus early on (I. ii. 39); and the words are an important clue. On the stage the barmecide feast scene is a grim parody of the Last Supper, and the scene at Timon's cave is much like the baiting of a hunted animal at its den: 'Get thee away, and take / Thy beagles with thee', Timon says to Alcibiades on his departure (IV. iii. 174): the beagles are the latter's attendants, including Phrynia and Timandra. Only the steward Flavus comes in a spirit of genuine affection (IV. iii. 457). The others' is lip-service; and their selfish ends show often and soon enough. The same is true of the visits of the Poet and Painter, and then of the Senators, early in Act V. Flavus makes the point perfectly clear. After all the suitors have come in vain, and immediately before the speech in which Timon gives warning of his own death, he says, 'Trouble him no further'. This has been the situation. The word 'beagles' had its point. Timon was 'hounded' if not to, at least until, his death.

VIII

SHAKESPEAREAN TRAGEDY
AND THE IDEA OF
HUMAN SACRIFICE

IT IS CLEAR, from the preceding chapters, that a certain
pattern runs recurrently through the tragedies discussed in this
book. This pattern has as its centre a very distinctive rôle pursued by the protagonist over the whole course of the play: a
rôle which takes him from being the cynosure of his society to
being estranged from it, and takes him, through a process of
increasing alienation, to a point at which what happens to him
suggests the expulsion of a scapegoat, or the sacrifice of a
victim, or something of both. Clearly, the pattern receives
different emphasis in different plays, and is less prominent in
some than in others. In *Hamlet*, for example, it is relatively
inconspicuous; though by no means absolutely so. Clearly
again, the details of its development vary greatly as between
one play and another. It is complete, in essentials, well before
the end of *Timon*; it does not begin to develop until long after
the beginning of *Coriolanus*; it is very much less explicit, and
less comprehensive in its application, in *Othello* than it is in the
later tragedies; and these are matters which very directly
affect the impact and value of these plays. But the present
chapter does not aim at an exhaustive relative evaluation of
Shakespeare's tragedies. Nor is it a general conclusion to the
present book. Most of what has been said already is unaffected

by its validity or otherwise. Its aim is to examine the interest of this one aspect of the tragedies: their partial resemblance to such scapegoat or sacrificial ceremonies as have been wide-spread in human society. It thus fulfils the promise given at the close of the Introduction. That promise, it will be noted, was to attempt the enquiry, not to succeed in it. What is said here is obviously tentative, certainly incomplete, doubtless in part erroneous.

First, the present enquiry is not a general one into 'tragedy'. Plays which, to a greater or lesser extent, suggest this same analogy with scapegoat or sacrifice may indeed be found out-side Shakespeare: Ibsen's *Brand* seems to be one of them. But they are not particularly numerous among the whole class of plays usually termed tragic. At most, this is one among several types of tragedy, a type towards which certain plays to a greater or lesser extent tend. Moreover, it must be associated to a quite special degree with Shakespeare. The majority of his tragedies are more or less plain examples of this trend; which in its turn could not be illustrated so readily, or clearly, outside his work. We are discussing something peculiarly, though **not** uniquely, Shakespearean.

It may be necessary to make this fact clearer. Every tragedy or near-tragedy is a serious play, in which the characters, in-cluding the protagonist, are likely to speak earnestly about the world, about how it works, or about how they would like it to do so. Every tragedy must start with a protagonist whose career ends in disaster: of necessity he cannot start there. Every dramatic character who is overtaken by disaster is likely to speak grandiosely when prosperous, and intemperately later on. Every such character must be in a weaker position at the end than at the beginning, and weakness easily means isolation. These are facts which may produce a partial resemblance to the pattern of tragic development in Shakespeare; but it is likely to be a superficial resemblance, one made up of shreds and patches, chance in its effect and superimposed upon a play where the central movement is of another kind.

Thus Sejanus, in Jonson's play of that name, is courted and toadied to at the beginning of the work; he once speaks vaunt-ingly and grandiosely in the course of it; he invites, at least at one point, a curse on the whole of Nature; he is conspicuously deserted and isolated in the Senate at the moment of his fall; and we are told that in the end he is torn to pieces by the common people. But these things combine with others in the play to produce a quite distinct and un-Shakespearean kind of totality. From the first, the comments of characters like Silius and Arruntius constrain the audience to see Sejanus as not a man of genuine if aberrant greatness of mind, but merely as an ambitious and power-loving careerist. He is a sharp contrast with the Shakespearean protagonist: an Edmund rather than a Lear. He undergoes no true ordeal of suffering and persecution, for his transition from complete power to complete ruin is reserved for the almost closing minutes of the play, and is then over almost at once. It follows from this that no response on his own part to the disaster which overtakes him can figure in the play; indeed, when he falls, Sejanus says nothing significant at all, his last speech being merely an insignificant wheedling gesture towards his overthrower. The nearest that the play approaches to depicting him in adversity is his speech at the end of Act V scene iv, after the false alarm which precedes his real fall; and if this goes beyond being one more boasting speech, it does so only vaguely and trivially.

The 'false alarm' has its own considerable interest, because it draws attention to what makes up the staple of this play; something utterly different from the staple of a Shakespearean tragedy. What sustains the interest of the audience is not the rôle pursued by the protagonist in both its outer and its inner aspects, but the twists and turns of a public struggle for power played out by rival factions—three rather than two, for Tiberius must be seen as in the game and playing his own hand. 'Who will win?' is the question constantly sustaining the tension and interest—or perhaps, since the audience knows from the title and the fact that the play is a tragedy, that Sejanus must lose, 'How can Sejanus be out-manoeuvred?'

We touch here, in fact, upon another kind of fundamental sustaining interest present in many plays both tragic and otherwise: that, in its simplest form, of the duel. The volume of the play is occupied by a struggle for power. The interest is sustained through our constant awareness of the question, who will win, or how will they win, or how can they win. The work is tragic in the sense that the losers meet disaster. This kind of interest is prominent in plays as different as *Julius Caesar*, *Andromaque* and *The Spanish Tragedy* (though it is not all-important in any of these). It is a kind of interest which can co-exist with the very different interest central in a Shakespearean tragedy; and our interest in the outcome of the struggle between Antony and Octavius, or Macbeth and the sons of Duncan, illustrates this. Merely to advert to such matters, though, confirms their relative unimportance in *Antony* or *Macbeth*. In *Hamlet* the situation is rather different. The tension of the struggle for power seems to run rather more prominently alongside the interest of Hamlet's personal ordeal; and the play, for all its integration and brilliance, is perhaps a less profound experience for us as a result. It is inadequate to call *Hamlet* a revenge tragedy, but it certainly has a great deal of the revenge tragedy in it.

It is plain enough that the main tragedies of Shakespeare move in a very different direction from *Sejanus*, or from any play where a struggle, a duel, is the centre of interest; but it makes sense to see this difference with the help of such ideas as ordeal or human scapegoat or sacrificial victim[50] only if what is truly helpful in these ideas is detached as sharply as possible from what is not. It would merely parody the present train of thought to suppose that, because both Gloucester and Macbeth speak of themselves as being tied to a post, being tied to a post has in itself some special significance; or that because both Lear and Coriolanus speak of themselves as dragons, seeming like a dragon was the essential point; or that any other such particular fact could be an essential constitutive part of the kind of dramatic movement now under consideration. What is genuinely constituent is the *type* of which these are *exempla*: in the first place, our impression, recurrent in play after play, of a protagonist who (to employ a metaphor) is hunted until he reaches a point where he can only turn and give himself up to the forces pursuing him; and in the second, our impression of how a protagonist who at first is a grand example of the human, becomes in the course of play after play set apart from the human, and in a very distinctive sense of the word (which itself constantly occurs) a 'monster'. It is this kind of generic movement, underlying each and every particular expression of it, which is at issue.

At this stage one must remind oneself of what was said at the close of the Introduction. What is now to be examined is a new metaphor through which certain plays may be seen; a comparison from which the current coin of criticism has forcefully averted notice, but which seems to be illuminating. The point may also be put by distinguishing the present question more exactly. It is not, 'are these tragedies "really" or "in effect" scapegoat or sacrifice rituals?' That they were, would be something which no literary critic is qualified either to assert or deny. It would be a matter to be determined by the exact definitions of certain terms employed by anthropologists or sociologists, and by the facts of social and cultural life, as they transpired in this or that society under examination.

The question to be discussed here is a different and on balance much less ambitious one. It is this: given a likeness (generic rather than particular, but unmistakable none the less) between the total movement of these plays, and rituals such as I have referred to, what in the plays as literary works does this throw into relief? The reference to the plays as literary works is to be understood as a reference to the experience offered by the work to a potential reader or audience: a reader or audience capable of responding to the interest that the work offers, of sensing the extent of that interest, and at the same time of bearing in mind its limits or even in some more positive sense its deficiencies.

Another possible difficulty must also be cleared up. In the earlier chapters of this book, actions by the protagonist such as proposing to divide the kingdom, enlisting under the powers of evil, invoking maledictions upon the whole of Nature, or being, by well-marked stages, isolated from the other *dramatis personae*, were several times referred to as 'formalized' or 'ritualized'. Since none of these actions is connected in any direct way with sacrificial 'ritual', it might be thought that the two parts of the discussion, and the two senses of the word, were devoid of any genuine link with each other. This is not so. The formalized and ritualized quality of the scenes examined was important because it helped the audience to see those scenes as not issuing by simple and all-directing causality from 'character', but as representing the more or less deliberate choice by the protagonist to live his life henceforth on a pattern which in part overrides character: to assume a rôle in which characters of many kinds could find their account. If we ask why this is so, the answer seems to be something like this: that the rôle in question embodies one of the major standing possibilities of human life. There are innumerable standing possibilities in life; but this is one—one, doubtless, among a number—of outstanding interest, one capable of engaging the attention, emotions and sympathy of the audience to an outstanding degree. Why is this so? This is the point at which the resemblance with sacrificial ritual, which the later chapters of the book have revealed, becomes relevant. What we have found in the plays is not merely behaviour by the characters formalized into something that goes beyond 'just behaviour' to be a more or less recurrent rôle to be conceived of in itself. We have also found that it has a clear if generic resemblance to an almost uniquely widespread communal institution. If we wish to find out why the recurrent pattern of development in the plays has a special significance for us, what is more to the point than to examine its resemblance to something which has clearly also had a special significance for mankind at large, and about the significance of which a body of opinion already exists?

Four points—to anticipate the findings of the rest of this chapter—must now be made. First, it is clear that some of the functions often seen in rites of human sacrifice have no parallel whatever in literary works; and that in these respects no light whatever is thrown on the latter by comparing the two. Second, there are certain aspects of the rites which possibly have their analogy in the works, and which it would be rash to dismiss out of hand; but that is as far as one can go. Third, there are certain other respects in which the analogy seems truly fruitful and suggestive; and leads us, as we might otherwise well not be led, to perhaps important potentialities in the tragedies. Fourth, there are one or two further respects in which the works and the rites are clearly distinct, but the distinction is not one of simple unrelatedness. It is that the works seem to be an extension or elaboration of the rites; seem to realize potentialities in these which they themselves have not realized—or if they have, it has been because a ritual tradition, over the course of history, actually transformed itself into a literary one.

The first of these four points may be dealt with briefly. Insofar as a sacrificial rite is a gift to a god, either placatory (i.e. 'piacular') or of a more general kind, it has nothing to do with our actual or potential experience either of Shakespeare's tragedies or of anyone else's. The same may at once be said of such functions as sustaining the society's food supply, keeping off inclement weather and the rest. These aspects of ritual performances have no bearing upon our discussion.

With other kinds of significance which have been seen in scapegoat or sacrificial rites (in practice and by nature, the two naturally converge upon each other) the position is different. This remains the case, even though no specific or detailed facts can be brought forward to show that in these respects the rites throw light upon literature. At this point, a further distinction must be made. The essence of a scapegoat rite is that the evil in a particular society is transferred to a certain individual, and then eradicated from the society through his destruction or expulsion. The participants do not of course believe that this happens merely in the sense that they have a conviction of its happening. They believe that it does so as a matter of objective fact. Others, however, who did not believe in the cult in this sense, could accept the effectiveness of the rite in a modified sense. If a social group is filled with the conviction that evil has been eradicated from it, there is a sense in which evil has indeed been eradicated, and the rite has been, to that degree, effective.

Something similar is true of another recognized view about the function of the sacrificial rites: that the shedding of life has been taken to be not simply a reduction of the forces of life, but a re-invigoration of these forces as well, in that (leaving irrelevant ideas aside) the vital energy of the victim is redistributed among those he leaves behind. The idea has been clearly expressed by E. O. James:

The fundamental principle throughout [the history of sacrifice] is the same: the giving of life to preserve life: death being merely a means of liberating vitality. . . . In all the manifold variations of the ritual the underlying significance consists in the setting free of life for one or more of the following reasons: (a) [to augment the power of the god or spirit . . .] (b) *to meet the forces of death and destruction by a fresh outpouring of vital potency, and to strengthen the worshipper* . . . (c) to establish or re-establish a bond of union or covenant with the benevolent powers in order to maintain a vital relationship between the worshipper and the object of worship. . . .[51]

The question now is, whether these aspects of scapegoat or sacrificial rites have a relevance for the tragedies under discussion.

Is not one's immediate inclination to answer, Surely not? Civilized persons today, it will be said, believe neither that evil in society may be transferred to a victim and eradicated from society by his expulsion or destruction, nor that anyone's vital forces are so released by death as to be distributable among his survivors. Neither of these convictions can have any proper part in our experience, actual or potential, of a tragic play; if, for any members of the audience, they did have such a part (even unconsciously), one would merely be obliged to infer that the experience of those members was atavistic. The matter is perfectly simple.

Strong as the inclination may be to believe this, and high as the probability may be that in fact it is true, there is one thing to say on the other side. Perhaps one could be a little too precipitate in dismissing these possibilities, in scornfully insisting that they could have no relevance to the civilized man's response to tragedy. I do not wish to claim that they positively have such relevance, nor even to suggest how, if they did have it, that might work out in detail. But even so, ideas of this kind at least harmonize with an adequate conception of what a great dramatic work is, and what kind of place it can occupy in the life of the culture to which it belongs. Were we to see a tragedy as operating on its audience, or being capable of operation, along either or both of these lines, we should at least be seeing it as a great emotional and imaginative force striking down to the deepest levels of personality, operating in ways too numerous and intuitive for us easily to distinguish, and veritably transforming its recipients through its regenerative and revitalizing powers. We should at least be far from that jargon of analysis and discrimination, defining and elaborating, questioning and explicating, which proved to have a certain radical inadequacy, to be out of scale with the great literary work. Our claims might be unsubstantiatable, and might well be incorrect; but they would at least not be disproportionate to that of which they were made. They would be right, rather than wrong, in kind, if not in fact. This is of course far from a sufficient reason for accepting them; but it is something of a reason for not straining too eagerly to reject them out of hand.

The next point to be considered comes much nearer to Shakespearean tragedy. It is the view, for example of Hubert and Mauss, that such rites as are now under discussion have as one of their chief functions to establish a relationship between those who take part in it, and the world of unseen and holy powers:

Mais si le sacrifice est si complexe, d'où peut lui venir son unité? C'est qu'au fond, sous la diversité des formes qu'il revêt, il est toujours fait d'un même procédé qui peut être employé pour les buts les plus différentes. *Ce procédé consiste a établir un communication entre le monde sacré et le monde profane par l'intermédiare d'une victime, c'est-à-dire d'une chose consacrée détruite au cours de la cérémonie.*[52]

W. Robertson Smith, who had already advanced a rather similar view, made it clear that although rites with this kind of efficacy originally took the form of a ritual feast in which the victim was eaten by the worshippers, the significance might survive in rites of sacrifice where this was absent; and also drew attention to a level of awareness at which the sacred is not seen as standing in sharp contrast to the world of Nature, but as an aspect, an intensification, of that world itself.[53]

Shakespeare's major tragedies are not in any way overtly religious works, as *Samson Agonistes* is an overtly religious work; and it is clear that if we are willing to use the word 'sacred' only in the overtly religious kind of context, they may be (indeed, are) the work of a devout man, but they do not offer their readers communion with the sacred in this sense. Less explicitly, however, they do seem to offer this kind of communion; and they do so in part through the very movement of dramatic interest which has emerged in the course of this book as a whole. The point must be put in fairly general terms. Repeatedly, the tragic protagonist in these plays is one who has moved from a position at the centre of well-ordered human life, to a position in which he is alien to that, in essence opposed to it, allied to what is enemy to it. Parallel with this, the protagonist passes through an ordeal of suffering which brings him from prosperity to death, but it is not death seen merely as one of the fortuitous hazards of life; it is seen from the start as the proper, and over the course of time as becoming almost the chosen, end of life lived as the protagonist has lived it. Life and death, or the forces which sustain life, and those which are enemy to it, are seen through the protagonist's career not in chance juxtaposition, but in a prolonged and intimate inter-penetration. Macbeth and Cleopatra must of necessity have seemed to have a consciousness of these matters, to encounter them, to engage with them, far beyond anything true of Sejanus. This is no accident, no gratuitous or super-erogatory enrich-ment by Shakespeare of his text; it follows, necessarily, from the very nature of the course which his protagonists pursue.

It would still be a catachresis to use such a term as 'the sacred' for such matters as these. But it is clear that if the tragedies tend of their very nature to turn the minds of their readers or audiences in these directions, they turn them in the direction of what is generally understood by that term. They turn them towards an apprehension of life seen in the context of what goes beyond life; of, one might say, the limits, and also the most essential livingness, of life. They do not do this in the sense of advancing a doctrine about these matters, but at a more radical level, that of opening the mind and directing the imagination. It would be naïve to infer from Shakespeare's drama that there is an 'order of nature' whereby men who live like Antony or Macbeth always, or normally, or indeed ever, meet the ends of Antony or Macbeth. Such inferences are about matters of fact, and they are to be drawn from another order of things than works of imagination. But to take stock of situations and careers such as theirs is to envisage life in a context of more than life. This remains true, even if when we are talking religion or philosophy, not literature, we conclude that expressions like 'more than life' and 'forces which sustain life or make against it' should be seen as having something of the metaphor about them, and decide that the word 'sacred', so far as we are con-cerned, points to something within the limits of humanity (or at least of Nature), not beyond it and in contrast to it. To employ an expression like 'the sacred' in a context so far removed from formal theology as this, may be to strain it; but the strain is one which is by now not unfamiliar; and may be seen, for example, in D. H. Lawrence's saying of himself, without a thought of organized religion or of any theology or creed, that he was 'a passionately religious man'.[54]

If the discussion is to be taken a stage further, certain further distinctions must be borne in mind. Anthropologists have seen sacrificial rites as creating a sense of communion not only between men and god, or more generally between men and some kind of sacred force which men sense in their whole environment; they have seen these rites as having also to do with a sense of community among the participants themselves. Durkheim has expressed this as follows: 'Les rîtes sont, avant tous, les moyens par lesquels le groupe social se réaffirme périodiquement.'[55]

A similar point had already been made, in less extreme form, by Robertson Smith:

... the case is very different when we look at the religious community as made up of a multitude of individuals, each of whom has private as well as public purposes and desires. In this aspect it is the regulative influence of ancient religion that is predominant, for the good things which religion holds forth are promised to the individual only in so far as he lives in and for the community. The conception of man's chief good set forth in the social act of sacrificial worship is the happiness of the individual in the happiness of the community, and thus the whole force of ancient religion is directed, so far as the individual is concerned, to maintain the civil virtues of loyalty and devotion to a man's fellows at a pitch of confident enthusiasm, to teach him to set his highest good in the prosperity of the society of which he is a member, not doubting that in so doing he has the divine power on his side and has given his life to a cause that cannot fail.[56]

Clearly, those who agree that religion in general, and sacrificial or scapegoat rites in particular, have as part of their effect the sustaining and strengthening of a social bond between those who participate in them, have room for disagreement on such matters as whether this social effect is the main interest of the rite, or is its ultimate historical source. But in these matters the student of literature need not take sides. Durkheim goes so far as to say of certain religious rites: 'C'est parce qu'ils servent à refaire moralement les individus et les groupes qu'ils passent pour avoir une action sur les choses.'[57]

Those who are religious in the plain sense are likely, and perhaps obliged, to deny this at least of their own rites. But for the
present discussion it is enough to notice how sacrificial rites are
generally recognized as having, *if only as part* of their effect
and value, an influence upon the social awareness and sense of
community of those who take part in them.

The central problem of this chapter—it is time to resume it—
relates to what constitutes the whole experience offered by such
tragedies as we have been examining; and it can now be seen
that to pursue the analogy between them on the one hand, and
rites of sacrifice on the other, is to conclude that a strengthening
and deepening of the spectator's sense of community with his
fellows may indeed be a major part of that total experience.
For consider what it is, upon which the attention of the audience
is fixed during the course of these plays—not so much in
Hamlet or even *Othello*, perhaps, but certainly in *Macbeth*, *Lear*,
Antony and Cleopatra, *Coriolanus*, *Timon*. It is fixed upon the
career and ordeal of a protagonist who makes, to adapt a well-
known phrase of Dante's, 'il gran rifiuto', the great refusal;
who progressively cuts himself off from the normal fabric of
human society and interdependence; who can say with Macbeth '. . . cancel and tear to pieces the great bond / That keeps
me pale', or with Lear 'I abjure all roofs', or with Cleopatra 'I'll unpeople Egypt', or with Coriolanus 'I banish *you*'.
Yet also, as the play proceeds, this great repudiator of the
common fabric of life is repudiated by what he repudiates; and
after a protracted ordeal of suffering which displays the full
measure of what it is that he has chosen as a way of life, meets a
death which is frequently accepted as appropriate for him both
by himself, and by those in the play who are most on his side.
We may recall Macbeth's words to the messenger after he has
threatened to hang him: 'If thy speech be sooth / I care not if
thou dost for me as much' (V. iv. 40); or Lear's 'If you have
poison for me, I will drink it' (IV. vii. 72); or Coriolanus's 'I
also am / Longer to live most weary, and present / My throat
to thee and to thy ancient malice' (IV. v. 94); or Antony's
'Unarm, Eros; the long day's task is done / And we must
sleep' (IV. xiv. 35). With regard to the acceptance of the
protagonist's death by those nearest to him, Kent's closing
words about Lear, and Iras's 'Finish, good lady; the bright

day is done / And we are for the dark' (V. ii. 192) are plain enough.

This acceptance is largely, I think, what gives the closing scenes of these plays their quality of sacrifice. Ordinary wishes and sympathies such as make up the normal fabric of life (or are commonly supposed to do so) are suspended, while the characters engage in the self-conscious completing of a recognizable kind of event, with such a validity of its own as sets it beyond considerations of pleasure and pain. Here is the note of ritual, of ceremony; and it is a ritual which enacts the destruction of one who, whether good on balance or evil, repudiated the bond of man to man. It enacts that destruction as (what in rites of sacrifice it has been and must be) accepted by the victim and his attendants as much as by anyone else.

I must now suggest—what is surely obvious—that a deep sense of community with others, as the basis if not the essence of human life, is not confined to primitive societies such as have sustained and strengthened this sense by (among other things) rites of sacrifice. It is a major part of the consciousness of men in any society. It is an intimate part of the being of us all. Only at the surface does it exist as convictions which most naturally assume a verbal form; and only on rather special occasions is it a matter of 'emotions' in the sense of gushes and suffusions of feeling. The sense of 'being members one of another', taken at its fullest, must be seen as a wide range of dispositions, of capacities for behaviour and for consciousness, stored within each individual, and taking the form when elicited of emotional disturbance, of heightened responsiveness and awareness, and of insight or intuition which is fuller, deeper, more spontaneous and less rigidly delimited, than what may readily be put into words. It is a whole realm of our personality, of our potentialities of life, which may be sensitized by this or that within our experience, but which is too large in scale, and too elusive in its ramifications, for the extent of its sensitization to be something of which we are necessarily or clearly aware.

Is it not now reasonable to suggest that to watch the full and measured enactment, in one of these tragedies, of a movement of events such as has been defined, does indeed elicit and awaken this side of ourselves? That a truly major part of the whole experience of such a play is the comprehensive stirring and calling to life of this whole side of our personalities? There may indeed be something speculative about this suggestion, and many may hesitate to agree that, for them, this is indeed part of the experience of the plays. Yet to say, on the other hand, that such a comprehensive awakening of one whole side of ourselves is merely part of the experience *offered* by the plays seems to fall a little short of adequacy; and I am inclined to suggest that this is not merely offered, but actually undergone, by many in their response to the actual occasion of a play's being read or being seen on the stage. If one hesitates to admit this, it may be less because it is no part of one's experience hitherto, than because of necessity it cannot but be an experience which spreads so wide and goes so deep that it is not readily identified.

That this may be common to several of the plays does not, of course, make against there being major differences in what they offer us as experience in other respects. Some of these have emerged already in the discussions of individual plays. But if the arguments were left at this point, it would expose itself to a forceful objection, a kind of *reductio ad absurdum*. For it might be said that the particular thread of interest which had been distinguished in this discussion merely suggested that Shakespeare, at the height of his powers and in a sense as the crown of his achievement, had created a kind of drama of which the most interesting thing one could say was that it performed a function such as those performed by the inhuman ceremonies of the Aztecs or the ritual activities of the Australian bushmen in respect of the Witchetty grub. This would win at best a grudging consent.

Perhaps it is not inappropriate, in the present context, to take the discussion a step further by quoting Spenser's description of the intended sacrifice of Serena by the cannibal 'saluage nation':

> Then gan the bagpypes and the hornes to shrill,
> And shrieke aloud, that with the people's voyce
> Confuséd, did the ayre with terror fill,
> And made the wood to tremble at the noyce:
> The whyles she wayld, the more they did reioyce.[58]

It is a realistic picture. Over and over, what emerges from

accounts of sacrificial rituals is that the victim is intoxicated or drugged so that he does not bewail his fate or cry out at pain; or that at the moment of death he is suddenly withdrawn from the sight of the main body of the participants; or, as in Spenser's account, that a noise is made which, at least as part of its effect, will drown the cries of the victim. When this is not so (which is rare) another way is sometimes employed whereby the power of the ceremony may not be impaired by the growth of sympathy for the victim of it: his cries, or perhaps even his tears, come to be required by the ritual itself if its efficacy is to be at its greatest.[59]

But where rituals of sacrifice have muffled and concealed one great and central part of what they contain, the tragedies which concern us here do the opposite. To follow the experience of *Macbeth* or *Lear* or *Antony and Cleopatra* is to be asked not to ignore the consciousness of the central figure, but to dwell on that and absorb it, to have it at the very centre of our attention; to have it there, furthermore, not merely through expressive cries which are mere symptoms of distraction and agony, but through a speaking part, rich with the resources of language used as poetry, and articulating not only the protagonist's sufferings, but his whole condition of mind, his whole predicament: to see him, his past, the decisive choices he has made, the way in which he has come to be where now he is, both from outside him, and also as he sees them himself. Then, by sympathy (in the strict sense of that word), it is to enter into the whole state of mind which is his response to this seeing on his own part. Everything which the rite of sacrifice is at pains to conceal, the drama is by virtue of its nature as a fiction free to enact, and by virtue of its language empowered to elucidate and deepen to an extent beyond comparison.

Yet it would be quite inadequate to see this aspect of the plays as merely offering the audience an interesting insight into what it is like to be in a very unfortunate situation, as if this were but one situation among many. For once again, are not the matters enacted by the play such as to call forth a response in us which comes from what is deeply and universally a part of ourselves? Men do not have a sense of community, of how they themselves are one with others in a social fabric, of how commitment to this is among the great standing conditions of life, unmitigated and unalloyed. This is no more than the happier side of their social consciousness. They are also aware of the price exacted for this constant support and re-invigoration from their fellows. It is the price of resigning oneself to the constant partial frustration of one's own nature, because for the moment it cannot be satisfied along lines which the social fabric will permit. For an individual to belong to society is on one side a constant re-birth of himself from the resources of that society, from another a continual dying of the self at the instance of the whole. All of us, surely, know this. It is part of our coming to terms with life. If our own lives are fulfilled and satisfied, and we do not feel the shoe pinching, that should only quicken in us an awareness of how the same is far from true for all. Perhaps, indeed, it is the happy and satisfied man who can most freely admit the point. He has no cause for self-pity, and therefore need not distrust it as covert self-pity. He is able to see it as a simple fact about human gregariousness, one so simple that it could perhaps be deduced from first principles.

It is not, however, learnt by any such process. It is learnt from experience, and it is learnt by such manifold experiences, and over so long a period of life, that one would be hard put to it to say when the learning either begins or concludes. Because this is so, our sense of the exactions of society upon the individual is a pervasive one, just as is our sense of how we as individuals have a place in the fabric of society and are sustained by that fabric. It, too, becomes a deep and ramifying part of our natures; the two intuitions, the two awarenesses, are counterparts of each other. What now emerges is this: it seems as if, in spite of the conflicting nature of the two, the experience offered us by the plays which have been discussed must, to something like an equal extent, evoke both. If this suggestion is right, the situation is a remarkable one. It must mean that the plays call forth in depth not only our sense of belonging to a community and drawing our strength from that, but also, and again in depth, all that is most naturally obscured when that awareness is kindled: all that reminds us of the price exacted for belonging, in the shape of constant partial self-abnegation. It is not, of course, that we see our own situation simply reflected in that of the protagonist. Ordinary and harmlessly conforming people do not find their lives plainly reflected in the situations of the great and greatly aberrant. But the more fully that the protagonist's predicament as he sees it himself, and the more fully that his response to that predicament, are articulated in the text, the more do we find ourselves confronted by a spectacle which may go much further than anything in our own lives, but which for all that must resonate deeply with what has been grafted into our natures by the experience of years. Our sense of the validity of community, and also the obverse of this, all that is most naturally thrust to the back of the mind when that is brought to the forefront of it, are called forth together. The experience comprises the excitation of two major parts of our whole nature, an excitation peculiarly comprehensive, ordered upon an antithesis peculiarly far-reaching in us and peculiarly definite in itself.

The distinction drawn so far between a rite of sacrifice, and a play like *Lear* or *Antony and Cleopatra*, has had regard to the greater inclusiveness of the one as against the other. Important as that distinction is, it is one of degree rather than of kind. Another distinction is more fundamental, in that it exists between the essential natures of the two things. It may be put in the form of a paradox, by saying—contrary to what one might inclined to say—that there is a sense in which the ritual is 'staged' and the play is not. In the ritual, the central figure is at first made the cynosure of all, dressed and treated like a king or a god, perhaps allowed to act with a freedom and an egotism out of the question in normal life, later both honoured and baited at one and the same time, and finally brought, through an ordeal of suffering, to a ceremonialized death. This may conceivably hold the attention of its participants, to some extent, because (though they do not realize it) such a sequence of things strikes unnoticed chords in their more normal experience. But if so, this is by the way. Seen as it is in itself, the ritual is unique. It reflects nothing, it imitates nothing. If, for its participants, it re-vitalizes quotidian life, it does so by standing outside that, not by being a part of it. Figuratively as well (often enough) as literally, it is extra-calendrical. It may work, but it does not point, beyond itself.

The plays which have concerned us make a total contrast. If they conform, inconspicuously but in essence, to the curve of movement of the sacrificial ritual, and if they have taken this further, in awakening for us also that inner life of the protagonist which the ritual carefully obscures, they have done these things within the setting of something entirely different. They have done them through the medium not of an enactment unique in itself and with no apparent relation to the rest of life, but one which has been a rich, elaborate and detailed representation of life. With Shakespeare's major plays, repeatedly, this representation is not only (as everyone will be quick, of course, to insist) unsurpassed in its quick and deep penetration into human nature. It also greatly surpasses the work of other dramatists in its range: in its power to take in most kinds of human behaviour from the solemn to the flippant, and most corners and varieties of human society. All this is obvious enough. It is also obvious that the point is entirely unaffected by Shakespeare's writing poetic and not 'Naturalist' drama (what is an exact surface reflection of life is exactly what will not bring out the things that that surface accidentally or deliberately conceals).

But it must be borne in mind that insofar as the plays are a representation of life which is also a comprehension of it, they are so, on account of something much more emphatically relevant to the present discussion than, simply, Shakespeare's sense of human or moral *value*. There is, indeed, no sharp contrast to be drawn between representation and comprehension by means of this term alone. Knowledge of what is good and evil in life is so much an integral part of knowledge of what life itself is, that the latter is in the most straightforward sense incomplete and defective without the former; and a written representation of life which was not a representation of some of the values in it, and therefore a comprehension of it in relation to values, could barely exist at all. Certainly it is possible to argue that the tragedies offer to do more than represent life— offer truly to comprehend it. But the distinction is barely a significant one unless we have more than moral values in mind as constituting the difference.

To have something further in mind, however, is not difficult. We realize what this is, as soon as we recall ourselves from the current coin of Shakespeare criticism, to think of how we use expressions like 'he comprehends life', 'he understands life', in our ordinary dealings with other people. The fact is, that these expressions point less to any sense of what are the basic values of life, than to a sense of how, at the most radical level, life works. What, that is to say, are its main lines of force; what kinds of action we can expect to succeed, what to fail; what is likely to be, in the ultimate future, the outcome of deeds known now only in their small beginnings. It is to know these things that is to know life, to comprehend life.

I think it is at precisely this point that the sacrificial rhythm which has been traced in the tragedies most forcefully relates them to the general course of life. This is so, because the rhythm itself, in its working out from beginning to end, simply *is* the ordering line of seemingly inevitable development under which the play offers to comprehend the major lines of force of life, so far as they enter into the area of life it represents. What 'orders' the representation of life through which the movement of hubris, alienation, dehumanization, retribution and sacrifice runs, is that very movement itself. Shakespeare's comprehension of life in *Macbeth* is that he who starts like Macbeth is likely to proceed and end as he does, taking his fellows and his society along with him; and insofar as, in following the play, we come to sense that this is true of Macbeth because of something that holds of life generally, that conviction is induced in us not by something extraneous to what happens to him, but by the integration, conclusiveness and seeming inevitability of that very movement itself. No literary work, of course, *proves* its view of life. If it did, it would not be a work of imagination. From the aspect of proof, indeed, the argument would move in a circle. What happens to Lear and Gloucester, we are left thinking, happens because the world is as it is and has the potentialities it has: but if we ask ourselves why we now see it in this light, the answer is nothing other than, because of what happened to Lear and Gloucester. From the standpoint of the work of imaginative literature, there is nothing whatever wrong with this: the function of such works is not to dictate ('life *is* like this') but to invite ('Is life not like this? Look at it again and see'). But the crucial point, for the present discussion, is that it is the sacrifice-rhythm of the tragedy itself, and nothing short of that, which the play advances as the principle ordering its representation of life, the principle by virtue of which that representation is also a comprehension. Such—so directly, so powerfully—is the way in which the rhythm of the dramas is not (as in sacrifice itself) a withdrawal from the ordinary patterns of our experience, but a returning of us into the very midst of them.

All this is to say that plays such as we have been examining do not (like the rituals themselves) suspend life in order to stage a ritual. They embed the essential movement of that ritual in life's common fabric. They *ritualize reality*. The general interest, no doubt, of a representation of life such as we find in these plays may be great in itself; but in the present context it is something more distinctive than this which has the main interest. This is, that because the ritual movement is embedded in a representation of life, and grows out of that, the double, deep response in us as audience which I have suggested that it excites is excited not of something which stands apart from life, but of something which points back to that: and does so with all the power of a work of art. The ritual sequence emerges from, and returns into, the world we know. It enacts and elucidates one of life's constant potentialities. Unlike the ritual, the tragedy does not stand in isolation. Insofar as it represents life, it brings us back to our own lives. This is an art which springs from reality, has its time of independence, and takes us back whence it sprang. The profound excitation of our natures which has been the effect of the plays is directed back upon the normal waking experience which is that nature's permanent source and guide.

APPENDIX A

DR LEAVIS AND 'DIABOLIC INTELLECT'

DR LEAVIS's *Diabolic Intellect and the Noble Hero: or The Sentimentalist's Othello* (in *The Common Pursuit*, 1952) is one of his most impressive and influential essays, and it undoubtedly shows some of his powers at their highest—shows, indeed, his genius. It is not quite enough to say this, however, without going on (as Dr Leavis does himself, in *The Great Tradition*, in respect of Dickens) to enquire exactly what kind of genius, what range of powers, is in evidence in it. The function of the present enquiry is thus to decide whether or not certain crucial steps in Dr Leavis's argument are cogent; and on the basis of its findings in this respect, to decide what kind of achievement the essay represents as a whole.

Chapter III of this book has shown that there is one important point, anyhow, at which *Diabolic Intellect* is wide of the mark. This is in saying (*The Common Pursuit*, p. 139) 'Othello has from the beginning responded to Iago's "communications" in the way Iago desired and *with a promptness that couldn't be improved upon*'. Admittedly, if the reader had to choose between this error (for error it is), and Bradley's steady under-rating of the strength and the evil of Othello's jealousy once he does become jealous; if, that is to say, he did not have Othello's own simple

> One not easily jealous, but being wrought
> Perplexed in the extreme;
>
> (V. ii. 348)

155

he would be in difficulty. If we have to choose between errors, we might prefer Dr Leavis's to Bradley's. Bradley's account is not only wrong, it is irritatingly so, and one cannot accuse Dr Leavis of blindness to this source of irritation. His responsiveness to it does not show, indeed, merely in asserting that Bradley tried to 'sentimentalize Shakespeare's tragedy and displace its centre' (p. 137). That comment is a just one. But it seems almost like praise of Bradley, by comparison with the abuse which runs, distractingly in my own experience, through the opening pages of Dr Leavis's essay. Bradley, we find, did not approach his task even 'with moderate intelligence' (p. 136); 'we must not suppose that Bradley sees what is in front of him' (p. 137); his essay is 'sustained and sanctioned perversity' (p. 138); Bradley and Coleridge together constitute 'as extraordinary a history of triumphant sentimental perversity as literary history can show' (p. 139); Bradley indulges a 'determined sentimental preconception' to heroic lengths, and (by implication) is 'protected by a very obstinate preconception' (p. 139); he wears 'blinkers' with a 'resolute fidelity' (p. 140). But no catalogue of quotations does justice to Dr Leavis's sustained note of exasperated sarcasm.

That note may be understandable; but—thanks to the dash and momentum of Dr Leavis's essay—we can by now afford to consider whether Dr Leavis, in his exasperation, replaced Bradley's errors by errors of his own; and it will transpire that the error which has already been noticed, that about Othello's 'promptness that couldn't be improved upon' or 'extraordinary promptness' (p. 144), is no isolated slip.

How much weight, for instance, ought we to set upon the defectiveness of Dr Leavis's arithmetic, at the point where he uses arithmetic to support his view of Othello's 'extraordinary promptness' in becoming jealous? Iago's sustained attack begins, he says, 'at about line 90 in Act III scene iii' (p. 144). In 70 lines, Dr Leavis continues, Othello is brought to such a state that Iago can warn him against jealousy, and use the word 'cuckold', but get no reply save 'O misery'; and in 90 lines Othello says 'Why did I marry?'. These two utterances do not come 70 and 90 lines, but 80 and 157 lines, from the point which Dr Leavis quotes as the beginning of Iago's attack. To those who say (justly) that little is proved by line-counting, the proper reply is not merely that it is with Dr Leavis that they must take issue, but also that there is one place, anyhow, in *Diabolic Intellect* where some line-counting would have been illuminating. This occurs a little later, in a discussion of the passage where Othello complains of a headache (III. iii. 286–93). 'Even the actual presence of Desdemona [writes Dr Leavis] . . . *can avail nothing* against the misgivings of angry egotism. Pointing to his forehead he makes an allusion to the cuckold's horns, and when she in her innocence misunderstands him and offers to soothe the pain he *rebuffs* her. The element of *angry sensuality* is insistent:

> What sense had I of her stol'n hours of lust?'

Why would some line-counting have helped? Because Dr Leavis does not point out that there is a gap between the passage he has been discussing (ll. 285–91) and the line that he quotes in illustration of Othello's 'element of angry sensuality' (l. 342). That gap is one of some 50 lines; during which Othello has left the stage and returned to it. This casts an uncomfortable light on Dr Leavis's word 'insistent'. After Othello's return, the note of that line is indeed insistent; but what of the passage, 50 lines earlier, which was under discussion? Here is the full text:

(Re-enter Desdemona and Emilia)

Oth: *If she be false, O, then heaven mocks itself!*
        I'll not believe it.
Des: How now, my dear Othello?
        Your dinner, and the generous islanders
        By you invited, do attend your presence.
Oth: I am to blame.
Des: Why do you *speak so faintly*?
        Are you not well?
Oth: I have a pain upon my forehead here.
Des: Faith, that's with watching; 'twill away again.
        Let me but bind it hard, within this hour
        It will be well.
Oth: *Your napkin is too little.*
        Let it alone. Come, I'll go in with you.
Des: I am very sorry that you are not well.

When the passage as a whole is read, there proves to be more ground for divergence from Dr Leavis's findings than simply that (whatever may be said of later passages) the 'element of angry sensuality' is certainly not insistent at this point. The word 'rebuff' may be suggested by the stage direction 'he puts the handkerchief from him, and she drops it', but this is a modern addition. 'Rebuff' is too strong by far for the text, in which Othello's note of courtesy or at least correctness, with something even of consideration for Desdemona, may not be all that is present, but cannot possibly be overlooked. As for her presence being able to 'avail nothing', against his 'egotism', this is clearly at variance (even should one—wrongly—concede that the word 'egotism' is just) with the very emphatic impact, conspicuous in the lines italicized, which her mere arrival has upon her husband.

I used the words 'dash and momentum' in describing *Diabolic Intellect*. These qualities are especially in evidence in one particularly difficult but particularly important passage (p. 145), for it is the passage in which the words 'egotism' and 'sensuality', the two main heads under which Othello's character is condemned, emerge fully in the discussion for the first time. Dr Leavis begins by a quotation:

> *Iago:* I would not have your free and noble nature
> Out of self-bounty be abused; look to 't:
> I know our country disposition well;
> In Venice they do let heaven see the pranks
> They dare not show their husbands; their best conscience
> Is not to leave 't undone, but keep 't unknown.
> *Oth:* Dost thou say so?
> *Iago:* She did deceive her father, marrying you;
> And when she seem'd to shake and fear your looks,
> She loved them most.
> *Oth:* And so she did.

and he continues:

> . . . And there, in the last line we have the noble and magnanimous Othello . . . accepting as evidence against his wife the fact that, at the willing sacrifice of everything else, she had made with him a marriage of romantic love. . . . Othello acquiesces in considering her as a type—a type outside his experience—the Venetian wife. It is plain, then, that his love is composed very largely of ignorance of self as well as ignorance of her: however nobly he may feel about it, it isn't altogether what he, and Bradley with him, think it is. It may be

love, but it can only be only in an oddly qualified sense love of her:
it must be much more a matter of self-centred and self-regarding
satisfaction—pride, sensual possessiveness, appetite, love of loving—
than he suspects' (p. 145).

This is a key passage, and every step in its argument must be
rigorous. The least sign of over-statement or hasty inference
here will be particularly damaging to Dr Leavis's point of view
of the whole. Because of this, it is disquieting to find Othello's
words 'And so she did' called 'accepting as evidence against his
wife'. The description is a little in advance of the text. All that
is clear from the text is that Othello has admitted that Desdemona loved him even in the early stages, when she was
actively concealing this from her father; what, if anything, is
to be understood by that is still an open question. By itself,
the point is a small one. It might not much matter even at so
crucial a juncture. But it does not come alone. For what is to be
thought of saying that in his reply to Iago's remark about 'our
country disposition', Othello 'acquiesces in considering (Desdemona) as a type—a type outside his experience—the Venetian wife'? All that Othello unmistakably does is to register that
he takes in, though with surprise, what Iago says. It is an inference even that he shows by these words that he acquiesces in
Iago's generalization. That he acquiesces in the further idea
that what is true of Venetian wives in general will be true of
Desdemona in particular, or, to go less far than this, that there
is even a fair basis of comparison between the general case and
this case, is a still more far-reaching, and still less probable
inference.

Dr Leavis's next sentence should also make the reader pause.
It is particularly condensed, and I find it far from easy to follow. 'Othello's love is composed very largely of ignorance of
self as well as ignorance of her.' Ignorant, in certain respects,
Othello doubtless is. He is ignorant of Desdemona in that he
does not dismiss Iago's insinuation from the first as (to say no
more) absurd. He is ignorant of himself (the point is something
of a logical quibble) if he overlooks—though that he positively
does so has yet to be proved—the fact that one Venetian wife,
his own, does indeed lie within his experience. Finally, if Dr
Leavis's argument is valid on other grounds, he is also ignorant

of himself, in not realizing a dangerous readiness on his part to tolerate or accept Iago's insinuations. Yet if he is in fact ignorant on these counts, it is still far from 'plain' that his *love* was largely, or at all, *composed* of that ignorance. To say that a man is in certain respects ignorant of himself is not to say that his love for another is in large part composed of that ignorance; the relation (if any, indeed) between love and ignorance is simply not that between whole and part.

Yet even now, the argument does not begin to run smoothly. Were we to make a gratuitous concession, and admit that Othello's ignorance of Desdemona, and of himself, were intrinsic to his love of her, and thus something that 'composed' that love 'very largely', the next step in Dr Leavis's argument would be as weak as the last. This next step is to assert: 'It may be love, but it can only be in an oddly qualified sense love of her.' Certainly, if that double ignorance were indeed what very largely composed the love, some qualification would be needed. But the obvious qualification would not be to say that Desdemona was the object of the love only in an odd sense; it would be to say that Othello's love for Desdemona was defective in quality. And at this point, after all these disablingly inconclusive steps in the argument, the reader arrives at the most obviously weak point in the whole of it: '. . . it must be much more a matter of self-centred and self-regarding satisfactions—pride, sensual possessiveness, appetite, love of loving—than he suspects.'

That 'must be', like the 'it is plain' which preceded it, is really an alarm signal. Even if it were right that Othello's love has an object which is not Desdemona, why 'must' that object be 'certain self-centred and self-regarding satisfactions'?—and even if it were, why 'must' these include sensual possessiveness and appetite? But the final weakness is not merely that these suggestions demand proof, and receive none. The situation is worse than that. The list bears signs, in respect at least of one phrase, that it has simply got out of hand. The phrase in question is 'love of loving'. It is a standard idiom to say, in certain cases, that a man's (especially a very young man's) ostensible love for a woman is not truly a love of her at all, but 'love of loving'. That what we have in mind in such a case, is also a part of Othello's case, will simply not bear inspection.

This examination easily could, and probably will, be called hair-splitting. Yet what short of it would reveal the extraordinary dexterity by which *Diabolic Intellect*, at this point, carries its reader forward, with what seems like irresistible cogency, through an argument which falls short of cogency at every single step? To see that the dash and momentum of the discussion, at this point, covers a sequence of argument which is uninterruptedly fallacious cannot but be laborious: such labour is the price we pay for brilliant aberration. Elsewhere the task is a little less laborious, but only if the findings of *Diabolic Intellect* are set against the full text of the play. The emphasis in that last sentence must fall upon the word 'full'; with all the inconvenience which that brings. Dr Leavis, for example, repudiates Bradley's stress on how Othello said 'O Iago, the pity of it, Iago' (IV. i. 191), by writing 'It is Shakespeare's tragedy of Othello that the man who exclaims this can exclaim three lines later, when he next speaks: "I will chop her into messes. Cuckold me!"' Again, Dr Leavis quotes from 20 lines or so earlier

I would have him nine years a-killing. A fine woman! A fair woman! a sweet woman!

and adds (p. 147) 'it is plain here that "fine", "fair", and "sweet" apply, not to Desdemona as a complete person . . . but to her person in abstraction from the character of the owner'. As it stands, the quotation does indeed seem to confirm the 'association of strong sensuality with ugly vindictive jealousy' which *Diabolic Intellect* castigates.

Do these damaging interpretations survive confrontation with the full text? Here it is:

Iago: And did you see the handkerchief?
Oth: Was that mine?
Iago: Yours, by this hand. And to see how he prizes the foolish woman your wife! She gave it him, and he hath given it his whore.
Oth: I would have him nine years a-killing. A fine woman! A fair woman! A sweet woman!
Iago: Nay, you must forget that.
Oth: Ay, let her rot, and perish, and be damn'd to-night; for she shall not live. No, my heart is turned to stone; I strike it, and it hurts my hand. O, the world hath not a sweeter creature; she might lie by an emperor and command him tasks.

Iago: Nay, that's not your way.

Oth: Hang her! I do but say what she is: so delicate with her needle, an admirable musician—O, she will sing the savageness out of a bear!—of so high and plenteous wit and invention.

Iago: She's the worse for all this.

Oth: O, a thousand, a thousand times—and then of so gentle a condition.

Iago: Ay, too gentle.

Oth: Nay, that's certain. But yet the pity of it, Iago! O, Iago, the pity of it, Iago!

Iago: If you be so fond over her iniquity, give her patent to offend; for, if it touch not you, if it comes near nobody.

Oth: I will chop her into messes. Cuckold me!

Iago: O, 'tis foul in her.

Oth: With mine officer!

Iago: That's fouler.

Oth: Get me some poison, Iago—this night. . . .

Dr Leavis has not extracted wisely from this longish passage. It is evident that Othello is oscillating violently between two sharply contrasting states of mind; and in quoting 'I will chop her into messes' and 'get me some poison, Iago' (with the words which follow) as throwing light upon the true nature of 'the pity of it', Dr Leavis has quoted from the one state, as throwing light on the other. This might not necessarily be wrong. The sharp contrast between them might be apparent only. We might be meant to see them as ultimately not very different (a little, for example, as Angelo's somewhat sadistic amorousness, in *Measure for Measure*, seems closely entwined with his anti-amorous repressiveness). But whether or not this is so is precisely the point at issue. It cannot be assumed as a basis for quoting from the one state of mind in order to throw light upon the other, for it is what has to be proved; and once this is seen, it is very surprising that Dr Leavis should quote 'I will chop her into messes' or 'get me some poison (etc.)' as having 'some bearing on the nature of "the pity of it" ', and not have drawn attention even to the existence of Othello's persistent harping upon Desdemona's skill with her needle or at music, her gift for singing, her witty and imaginative mind, her gentle (that is, high-born) origin—all of which do not have 'some' bearing upon 'the pity of it', but a great deal of very direct bearing.

In fact, it is not too much to say that with the whole text before him, the reader will see these as the expressions which cast light upon 'the pity of it', and '. . . cuckold me!' as not casting light upon that, so much as deliberately standing in sharp contrast to it. In uttering these words, Othello, oscillating violently between feelings for Desdemona which were once unimpaired, and newer feelings of brutal jealousy and vindictiveness, has swung (provoked, it will be observed, by Iago's taunt) from one extreme to the other. Moreover, the whole text sets Dr Leavis's comment on 'fine', 'fair' and 'sweet' in another light; for it is certainly not 'plain' (how these encouragements to agreement provoke scepticism, once their constant repetition is noticed!) that these words point to Desdemona's person in abstraction from her character, or display an association of strong sensuality and ugly vindictiveness in Othello. In the first place, they point to the sharp contrast which exists for Othello between the callous and lecherous Cassio (as Othello now thinks him), and what Desdemona at least was before Cassio helped to corrupt her. (At this point the reader should refer back to the opening lines of the long quotation above.) More specifically, they point, or at least 'sweet' points, to the fact that Othello thinks Desdemona fit (or once fit) to be bride to an emperor, and indeed be waited on by him. No one, I suppose, will be so extravagant as to think that the 'tasks' are meant to be tasks connected with 'strong sensuality'.

With the full text before him, the reader probably feels that some surprising omissions have been made, and that Dr Leavis's 'it must be' and 'it is plain' and 'this surely has some bearing' did not help his discussion as much as, presumably, he thought they did. But had the long quotation above been continued only a line or so further, it would have included a passage upon which *Diabolic Intellect* lays great weight:

Get me some poison, Iago—this night. I'll not expostulate with her, lest her body and beauty unprovide my mind again—this night, Iago.

(IV. i. 200–202)

These are lines upon which Dr Leavis lays such stress that he puts them to a perhaps disproportionate use: he quotes them twice over. Later in his essay (pp. 149–50), discussing the soliloquy of Othello's which opens Act V scene ii, he writes (my italics): 'Tenderness here is less specifically voluptuous sensuality than it was earlier, *but we nevertheless remember: "Get me some poison, Iago* (etc.)"'. That is to say, Dr Leavis uses this passage a second time, as if it were devastatingly conclusive, to cancel out the one passage he quotes which seems a little to make against his general case.

The words 'we nevertheless remember' do not mean that while actually watching or reading the play, we find ourselves, or ought to find ourselves, recalling just those words at just this point, on account of a reminder of them which Shakespeare has deliberately put into his text. They mean that in a critical examination and considered review of the play, we recall them as a corrective to the hint of 'tenderness' in the soliloquy; they prevent us from putting too great a weight upon the fact that tenderness here seems 'less specifically voluptuous sensuality than it did earlier'; and they prevent our falling into that error, because they themselves afford a decisive, an absolutely unambiguous link (or, if we give Dr Leavis's expression 'is . . . specifically' its proper force, equivalence) between the two.

Yet on reflection, these words do no such thing. What Dr Leavis takes as the decisive proof of how Othello's love is at bottom voluptuous sensuality is no proof at all. This is because—I take it that I am now about to repeat a commonplace—it is simply false that women's bodies and beauty unprovide men's minds through exciting 'voluptuous sensuality'. Here it is natural to prefer to speak with a certain reserve. Nothing is lost by so doing. It is enough to recall certain obvious facts of which the significance will be clear to every adult as soon as he or she begins to reflect. Desdemona is Othello's bride; she is young and beautiful; she has been his wife in the full sense, but for a very short time only; his love for her has indeed been violently destroyed, but he did love her, again in the full sense, until only a few hours ago. Now he is contemplating what his response will probably be, as he watches *her* responding to, and presumably defending herself animatedly against, his 'expostulation'; and it occurs to him that his expostulation might be suspended. What has all this to do with an insistent note of voluptuous sensuality? Nothing whatever. The words are grotesquely irrelevant. What is in question is what makes part of everyone's familiar knowledge about love, marriage and attraction between men and women. And since it would be out of the question to suppose that any of these simple facts are unknown to Dr Leavis—indeed, it is difficult to believe that they are unknown to anyone in normal health—we must therefore attribute his disregard of them, and his jumping to the conclusion that he had found evidence of voluptuous sensuality, only to that brilliant but distracting quality of his essay to which I have already referred. This is, the dash and momentum which carries it irresistibly—or almost so—along; at the constant price of hastiness and distortion.

Whether this recurrent hastiness and distortion are the products of Dr Leavis's not unnatural exasperation with Bradley, and eager desire to refute Bradley's findings, it is impossible to say. But this seems a not unlikely account of the note of vexation which runs throughout his piece, and of its bewildering omissions of quotation, its constant stress on one side and ignoring of the other, its constantly sharpening insistence upon a certain view of Othello's character, and above all, of the dash and momentum, the eager *brio*, which runs through it, sweeping the reader along, and making it difficult for him to see how the argument is advancing by steps which constantly fall just, or far, short of cogency. At this point, so it seems to me, one recognizes the distinctive range of powers which are at work in this piece. Everything which can be pressed into service to point one way is exploited with animation and zeal, everything else (save for one little scrap) buried and ignored. The whole brilliant piece is geared to the destruction of Bradley's case. The genius which it displays is a forensic genius; none the less so for being (I assume) forensic quite without intention. *Diabolic Intellect* does not display Dr Leavis's powers as a critic at their best; but for a display of his powers at their highest, *Diabolic Intellect* is perfect. It is no wonder that one may justly say of Dr Leavis what he said of Bradley, and assert that what he wrote 'is still a very potent and mischievous influence'. Probably it will survive this, and abler, examinations of it. That will not be for its merits as criticism.

APPENDIX B

THE CONCEPTS OF 'MYTH'
AND
'RITUAL' IN LITERATURE [60]

I

IT WOULD BE possible to express the views now to be put forward, in exaggerated or caricatured forms; these would be incorrect in substance and harmful, perhaps very much so, in tendency. This is true of all caricatures of all points of view, not least those which are most respectable and well-established. On the other hand, against this examination of the degree to which there may be parallels between works of the literary imagination and myth or ritual, one perhaps weighty objection may be brought. It is, that what is said here is other than what is said usually. For good or ill, the present discussion finds the essence of the literary work in something different from that in which today it is usually found.

Ernst Cassirer's *Philosophy of Symbolic Forms* (1925) is undoubtedly one of the major works of philosophical synthesis of our time. For those whose chief concern is the literary work of art, to read the second volume, *Mythical Thought*, is a disconcerting and suggestive experience. Cassirer's field of interest in this part of his book might be described as the mythologies—pantheons, creation stories and all that goes with these—of classical, Indian and (with help from the anthropologists) primitive cultures; and above all with what may be inferred of the cast of mind which could create these and see the world through them. He is thinking in general terms, and is at no point concerned with particular versions of this material such as is to be found in early or primitive works of literature. Yet for all this, his account of what he calls 'mythical thought' comes close, time after time, to what we know as the kind of thinking carried out by the creative writer. The student of literature who reads this volume finds his basic ideas about the literary art presented, one by one, in a quite fresh projection.

I shall confirm this, briefly and incompletely, by extracting three points from Cassirer's extended discussion.

First, Cassirer's idea of the essentially tentative, exploratory and creative nature of mythical thinking (italics in these quotations are mine):

Myth . . . does not start from a finished conception of the I or the soul, from a finished picture of objective reality and change, but must achieve this concept and this picture, *must form them from out of itself.* . . . The more widely we extend the scope of (the phenomenology of the mythical consciousness), the more deeply we penetrate its primal and fundamental strata, the more evident it becomes that for myth the concept of the soul is no stereotype into which it forces everything that comes within its grasp but is rather *a fluid, plastic element* which changes in its hand. . . . Primitive thinking is actually characterized by the peculiarly *fluid and fugitive* character of its intuition and concept of personal existence.

This is a passage in which Cassirer is discussing how mythical thinking has seen the individual psyche, but insofar as it gives an account of mythical thought itself, its application is intended by the author to be quite general; and the analogy with our own generally accepted ideas about the whole mode of apprehension of the artist, in contrast maybe with the scientist, is so plain that it needs no elaboration.

The second part of Cassirer's account of mythical thought which affords a link with literature is akin to the first. It is his account of how this kind of thinking does not analyse and separate, but naturally apprehends its material in the form of organically unified wholes:

. . . for the mythical imagination there is no separation of a total complex into its elements, but . . . only a single undivided totality is represented—a totality in which there has been no *'dissociation'* of separate factors, particularly of the factors of objective perception and subjective feeling.

or again:

another trait . . . has always been stressed as characteristic of the mythical world view, namely the peculiar relation it assumes between the *whole* of a concrete object and its particular *parts*. . . . Even where empirical intuition seems, of itself, so to speak, to give us inwardly differentiated things, myth replaces this sensuous separation and contiguity by a characteristic form of interpenetration. The whole and its parts are *interwoven* . . . anyone who acquires the most insignificant bodily part of a man—or even his name, his shadow, his reflection in a mirror, which for myth are also real parts of him—has thereby gained power over the man . . . the whole phenomenology of magic goes back to this one basic premise, which clearly distinguishes the complex intuition of myth from the abstract, or more precisely abstracting and analytical, concept.

The analogy with literary creation is not of course that the writer can see a man's shadow as his self. It is that this account of the mythical mode of apprehension is essentially the same as what we might give of the literary, or more particularly, the poetic.

That literature is exploratory-creative in approach and organically unified in its product are now commonplaces; and to say that if mythical thought has these qualities, it bears a likeness to literary thought, is to say what need barely be argued for. The third and last point of resemblance which is suggested by Cassirer's account requires closer consideration. It emerges when he says (following field anthropologists like Codrington in his work on the Melanesians) that, at least so far as the myth-maker himself is concerned, there is a very distinctive quality which tends to be possessed by what is made the subject-matter of the myth. This is the quality of *mana*. That word is not easily translated into English, though there appears to be a synonym for it in the languages of a number of primitive communities. It certainly does not mean what we mean by 'spiritual'. Cassirer gives a fuller account of the concept in another work, *Language and Myth*: all in all, it appears that many communities sense a quality common to whatever is outstanding, wonderful, mysterious, terrible, joy-bringing, striking or imbued with unusual power. The things which are seen to have this quality comprise the domain of myth.

Is not this very quality of things, the quality which seems to render them powerful, unique and memorable, one which writers of literature have notably, and recurrently, sought in their material?—'the golden world' of the poet (Sidney); 'a mere imitation will not serve' (Dryden); 'to see Eternity in a grain of Sand' (Blake); 'the loveliness and the wonders of the world before us' (Coleridge); 'the romance of common things' (Dickens); 'Experience is never limited and it is never complete . . . when the mind is imaginative . . . it converts the very pulses of the air into revelations' (Henry James); 'the boredom and the glory and the horror' (T. S. Eliot); 'life is not like that! . . . life is a huge and semi-transparent envelope . . .' (Virginia Woolf);—time after time, the writer serious enough to reflect on his art seems to have seen it as a pursuit of this resonance, this reverberation, which runs through much or the whole of reality. This is not, it will be understood, to advance a theory of literary composition. It is simply to notice what seems to be another respect in which Cassirer's account of mythical thinking affords an analogy with the processes of mind of the creative artist. By now this analogy looks very substantial.

II

In spite of its interest up to this point, there is something radically defective about Cassirer's whole discussion of myth, and the time has come to recognize what that is. Today indeed, and in this country, we are likely to be ill at ease from the very start with concepts so abstract as 'the mythical consciousness'; but the fact is, that Cassirer wrote before the time of field anthropology, and in spite of reacting from such thinkers in the field as Max Müller, his conception of the mythical is in general more aetiological and indeed more cognitive than the anthropologists' empirical studies will warrant. Malinowski's first study of the Triobrand Islanders appeared in the very year following Cassirer's *Philosophy of Symbolic Forms*: and he broke with Cassirer's *a priori* and Kantian approach to replace it by one which is detailed, empirical, and above all functional. For him, there is no 'myth' nor 'mythical consciousness', save by inference

from *activities* which are directly observed; and observed moreover in their living context, as they perform their distinctive
function within the whole complex of activities of a particular
society.

Malinowski found, in fact, that the society of the Triobranders
did not simply contain an element of 'myth', but several different activities of story-telling, with three easily distinguishable
kinds of narrative told communally according to certain forms
which were carefully observed in different ways, at different
times, and above all, for different but recognizable purposes.
Here in fact is the crucial difference, which might be summar-
ized by saying that a myth *does not so much talk, as work*. Its function is not so much to answer a question about the world—the
old-fashioned aetiological idea of myth—as to contribute to, or
sustain, some reality now current in the society. 'Myth . . . is
not an intellectual reaction upon a puzzle, but an explicit act of
faith born from the innermost instinctive and emotional reaction
to the most formidable and haunting idea.' Again, writing of
myths of the origin of the society or of men in general:

what really matters about such a story is its social function. It con-
veys, expresses, and strengthens the fundamental fact of the local
unity of the group of people descendent from the common ancestor.

and therefore:

the really important thing about the myth is its character of a retro-
spective, ever-present, live actuality. It is to a native neither a
fictitious story, nor an account of a dead past; it is a statement of a
bigger reality still partially alive. It is alive in that its precedent, its
law, its moral, still rule the social life of the natives. It is clear that
myth functions especially where there is a sociological strain. . . .
We can certainly discard all explanatory as well as all symbolic
interpretations of these myths. . . .

In writing in these terms Malinowski is merely the first (or
among the first) marking a general change to the point of view
of the anthropologist in the field instead of in the study. Marett
in 1932 wrote 'the myth is not aetiological but fidejussive: its
business is not to satisfy curiosity but to confirm the faith'.
Radcliffe-Brown, in his study of the Andaman Islanders,
pointed out that their myths could barely be for the purposes of

explaining the facts of nature, since they were not consistent. But

on the view that the myths of primitive society are merely the result of an endeavour to express certain ways of thinking and feeling about the facts of life which are brought into existence by the manner in which life is regulated in society, the presence of such inconsistencies need not in the least surprise us; for the myths satisfactorily fulfil their function not by any appeal to the reasoning powers but by appealing through the imagination to the mind's affective powers.

Finally, as a much more recent account, here is E. O. James, writing on the 'Nature and Function of Myth' in *Folklore* in 1957. Myths, he writes, are not the product of a mythopoeic mode of thought endeavouring to comprehend and explain the universe; but myths about such matters as the creation of the world, the round of the seasons, birth and death, and so on,

have taken shape round certain crucial events of permanent significance . . . in order to bring them into direct relation with the existing physical, cultural, social, ethical, and religious conditions and organization, and to stabilize the established order both of nature and in society, to confirm the accepted beliefs and customs, to vouch for the efficacy of the *cultus*.

III

This transformation of the concept of myth in primitive societies perhaps suggests certain insights in the field of literary studies. In a sense this is self-evident or even tautological; once we begin to think of myth not vaguely, as a mode of thought, but definitely, as an occasion of reciting a narrative, it is plain that we have already reached a literary event. But there is something which goes further than this, and offers insight into the nature of literature as it exists in advanced societies such as our own. To attempt to employ an insight gained from primitive societies in the comprehension of advanced societies and what goes on in them is hazardous, and one must be prepared for some inconspicuous but sharp differences. The myths of primitive society, for example, may indeed only strengthen and confirm an established organization: primitive societies are exceedingly static. More advanced societies (as sociologists have noted) may have resources for change actually built into their permanent organization; and if there is anything which functions, in them, analogously to myth in primitive society, it is unlikely to do *nothing* but attack and challenge the existing organization of life, but it is very likely to attack and challenge certain aspects of this from the standpoint of endorsing certain others. This may be the point at which to recall that literature by no means merely asserts established values. As much as doing this, it is one great challenger and disturber of them, and of the complacencies into which they easily lapse: one great source, as Shelley saw in his *Defence of Poesy*, of men's awareness that they may elevate life above what it has been already.

Again, it may very well be true that in primitive societies the myth performs its social function in spite of inconsistency of outlook, without offering answers to questions, or a formed view of the cosmos, and through an appeal only to the 'affective powers' of its hearers. This would not imply that the same function was necessarily performed in an advanced society by something with the same limitations. Still less, of course, would it imply the opposite. The situation would remain open for investigation. Nor should it be thought that these two points are likely to exhaust the differences which we are likely to encounter when we move from the primitive to the advanced; on the contrary, general experience should lead us to expect that qualifications will have to be made, unpredictably and from time to time, as the investigation proceeds.

Yet despite all these cautions, a significant fact remains. In the field of anthropology, there has been a revolution in the concept of myth. An earlier generation of scholars saw myths as a distinctive kind of attempt (specially valuable, or barbarous and limited as the case might be) to comprehend the universe, or the state of man, and to convey *implicit information*. There was a doctrine at the heart of the myth, even though it was expressed in the concrete form of a narrative. This sounds very like much recent discussion by literary critics of literary masterpieces. The parallel is a striking one, and a sociologist studying our own society might conceivably see both trends as illustrative, in their different ways, of some of the underlying forces or needs in it. But it appears that in the field of anthropology there has in recent years been a shift of view about myths. These are seen less as statements, than as agents, in their societies: less as offering explanations, than as exercising power. They are moulders, controllers and sustainers of how men live. This is an especially interesting shift of viewpoint, in that it seems not to have come alone. It runs in the same direction as recent shifts of emphasis in other intellectual disciplines. It is parallel, for example, to the recent movement in philosophy which has been summed up in the slogan, 'don't ask for the meaning, ask for the use'. 'Use,' in that context, has turned out to mean a range of different uses, and it has come to be recognized, with a new exactitude and detail, that some uses of words are to make statements, but others are to do this only in part, or even not at all. Other parallels could be found.[61] In the end it seems that in the newer point of view of anthropologists about myths there is something characteristic of intellectual enquiry in our time. That is not necessarily in its favour; but it adds to the interest, and perhaps to the significance, of the case.

If we infer that a shift of viewpoint in literary studies, parallel to the shift of viewpoint with regard to myth, might lead to valuable new insight and awareness, we should at the same time be careful not to go further than the situation warrants. Malinowski, Radcliffe-Brown and others have been outspoken in claiming that in anthropology the newer viewpoint renders the older one simply untenable. 'As to any explanatory function of these myths, there is no problem which they cover, no curiosity which they satisfy, no theory which they contain.' This is how Malinowski concludes one discussion of the Triobranders' myths of origin. It may perhaps be doubted even whether the alternatives in anthropology need to be posed quite so sharply as this. But in the literary field there is no reason whatever to suppose that if we attempt to exploit this newer viewpoint of anthropology with regard to myth, and consider some of our great imaginative works as sources of power and influence rather than information, as great sustainers and moulders of the cultural life of the community or the individual, we are therefore bound entirely to repudiate the view which sees them as expressing 'meanings', or suggesting answers to fundamental questions about the nature of Nature, man or human life. Certainly, this way of seeing the great imaginative work could no longer be considered as the only way, nor even perhaps the way which brought out most directly what distinguished the work, what made it what it was and not another thing. But it could certainly remain one aspect of its interest, and in fact these two ways of seeing the work could be brought together in any of several different combinations, into the details of which there is no need to go.

The point of view with regard to works of imagination which I have been suggesting by analogy with anthropological studies of myth is not, it must be admitted, very informative so far. It may be a way of seeing, but what is seen when this way is adopted has so far been left uncertain. In one respect, however, something has already been gained. Let us recall Johnson's remarkable description of the impact of *King Lear*: [62]

There is perhaps no play which keeps the attention so strongly fixed; which so much agitates our passions and interests our curiosity. The artful involutions of distinct interests, the striking opposition of contrary characters, the sudden changes of fortune, and the quick succession of events, fill the mind with a perpetual tumult of indignation, pity and hope. There is no scene which does not contribute to the aggravation of the distress or conduct of the action, and scarce a line which does not conduce to the progress of the scene. So powerful is the current of the poet's imagination, that the mind, which once ventures within it, is hurried irresistibly along.

To endorse these words almost in their entirety (as one must) is immediately to confront a problem.

It is not out of the question that a statement, a resolution of questions about the nature of man or the world, should be expressed or embodied in a form which evoked powerful and varied emotions; and certain parts, for example, of the Christian scriptures might be cited in this context, though their ultimate bearing on the discussion would prove an intricate one. Nevertheless, it is by no means what we should take for granted or most naturally look for; and it is clear that for the view of the great imaginative work which sees it as in the first place the expression of a meaning, here is something of the highest interest, something which very much demands explanation, and something of which the explanation is far from self-evident. Here, in short, is a difficulty. From the other point of view, the difficulty vanishes. That a signal source of mental or spiritual power and energy in a culture should prove to have a tremendous and varied emotional impact latent in it is exactly what we should predict. So far from this being a surprise, something of which we feel we should like to have the fullest and most exact account we can get, it is precisely what we are likely to feel least in need of explanation. It would be any other state of affairs which would present the problem and demand the explanation. To this extent, then, limited as it is, the point of view of the imaginative work which I have been developing by the aid of an analogy with myth seems to face in the right direction.

IV

There is an obvious objection, however, to this train of thought: that it has not provided an alternative answer to that of the critics who see the imaginative work's chief centre of interest as its meaning, but has provided no answer at all, in that it has shifted the ground of the discussion from the nature of the work merely to its effects. One may fairly say in reply, however, that a re-appraisal of the effects of something is often the right preliminary to a better knowledge of its nature. Ultimately there is no way of determining the nature of imaginative works other than perceptive apprehension of them; but I am sorry to say that a commonly held idea about how this may be done is a myth in the unhelpful sense of the word. It is, that there is something called the literary sensibility, which is perfectly equipped, and (or perhaps because) self-equipped, to recognize all that is present in the work. This is a conceivable but not actual state of affairs. The ground for saying so is our general knowledge of how men improve their powers of discrimination not merely by practice in discrimination itself, but also by extending their knowledge of the range of possible things among which they may have to discriminate. We see what we have learnt to know may be there to see. What observer, however sensitively his perceptions had been trained, could give a proper account of a bird perched on a tree, unless he already knew of birds as things which he might expect to see from time to time—and which flew?

With this in mind, one may recall the idea of the imaginative work as a source of power (an idea confirmed, it is now clear, by the work's effects), and consider whether there is not another idea which the literary scholar may borrow from the field of myth, and which may help him to recognize certain comparatively neglected features of things, or rather some things, in his own field. This idea is the idea of ritual. The profound, though intricate, and as regards its details controversial connection between myth and ritual for primitive or early societies has of course been considered by many workers or thinkers in the field of anthropology (Frazer, Jane Harrison, Lord Raglan and also Miss Weston, perhaps, are names which come to mind). The purpose of this discussion is not to resume or assess that body of work, but simply to start with a general recognition of this linkage, and to see whether, if it is allowed to play freely in the mind, it brings to light aspects of imaginative works which might otherwise elude critical observation. I shall not be arguing that imaginative works *are* rituals in disguise, nor (save of course for the cases like Greek tragedy or medieval miracle plays, where it is already common knowledge) that they derive from rituals or explain or justify them. Such extravagances would be absurd. Nor do I have in mind anything like, for example, what Francis Ferguson says in a discussion entitled *Hamlet as ritual and improvisation*; for what he sees as the ritual element in the play is that it frequently stages public ceremonies. The significant analogy between work and ritual proves to be much less complete and obvious, but also much more sustained and significant, than anything of that kind; and the crucial issue is whether recognizing an important though of course incomplete analogy between an imaginative work and a ritual may prove to sharpen our perception of the former—the imaginative work, our primary concern—so that we can apprehend its intrinsic qualities more fully or more justly.

This whole enquiry, that is to say, is to elicit something of the nature of the great imaginative work. This (like the myth) seems to be a source of power, of sustained, renewed or enhanced vitality, in the life of the community or individual, and it proves to exercise this power through effects, as Johnson reminded us, which are outstandingly moving and agitating. Certainly, the same may be said of some of the major rituals of any society; and with this in mind, there may be profit in reviewing some recurrent features of ritual and considering the work of imagination in the general light of them.

The basic distinction between a ritual and a myth, of course, is that the former is a δρώμενον, a thing carried out, a particularized activity; whereas a myth is not, in itself, even a particular narrative, it is something like a potential narrative, something which may be set forth in this or that particular occasion of narration. To notice this is already to have encountered something reminiscent of the difference between, say, the story of Lear (which has been told many times, in varying versions), and the play *Lear*, which is a unique and in a sense sacrosanct *transacting*, as it were, of that story.

This, perhaps, suggests another respect of resemblance between the literary work and the ritual. Ritual must, at every stage, be perfectly authentic. A defective version is no version: the virtue has gone out of it. Moreover, the authentic version must be executed through from beginning to end; it must not be abridged, its parts must not be transposed. To modify it in any such way is not an imperfect performance of the ritual, so much as an attack upon it, an affront, a blasphemy. What affords the analogy in the case of the imaginative work is not the strict demands of the textual scholar (though these, in the context, may take on a new interest) but the whole attitude of the serious but critically-minded reader to the reading of a great work: the rather distinctive nuance in how he would condemn skipping it (at least, skipping whole sections of it), leaving it unfinished, reading the end first, reading the book of the film or an abridgement or a simplified or modernized version. There is a tendency, surely, for us to reject the very idea of a 'version'. Rather, we are inclined to recognize, on the one hand, the authentic text, which—yes, which we almost revere; and, on the other, travesties which interest the enemies of the culture rather than its adherents. These may seem small points; but they cannot be ignored. It is by signs like these that the true status of something in our culture, the true place which it has in the spectrum of our lives, tends often to be revealed.

Two further points of resemblance between rituals and works of the literary imagination must now be mentioned, and they are more significant than those which have been mentioned so far. Many rituals, of course, are thought by their participants to have effects of a special kind. They bring rain, drive away spirits, or bring it about that human beings or their activities are associated with divine grace. There is, needless to say, no analogy along these lines between a ritual, and an imaginative work as it has a place in the lives of individuals in an advanced community. On the other hand, those who are not adherents of the ritual cult do not normally admit effects of this kind; but they recognize that even so the ritual is not without its effects, and that these are what give it a place of value in its society. These other effects are psychological effects which it has upon those who take part in it, or on others associated with them. They relate partly to the convictions and beliefs, more to the emotions, and most of all, it may be, to the dispositions, of those concerned. 'Sustained, renewed or enhanced vitality,' the words used some while ago about the effect of an imaginative work, well describe these effects of the ritual performance. If more could be said of what it is in the ritual which induces these effects, light might be shed upon what there is in the imaginative work which induces similar ones.

V

This brings the present discussion to the most speculative and dubious step in its argument. If it is valid, it considerably strengthens the whole train of thought; but if it is not valid, the train of thought does not for that reason collapse out and out. It merely carries less conviction that it might, which is a not uncommon state of affairs. The point at issue may best be reached by noticing what surely proves, on reflection, to be a very remarkable and intrinsically improbable fact about outstanding narrative works, whether dramatic or in the form of prose or verse fiction, throughout history. It is a fact so simple that it seems not to have received the attention it deserves. When brought out, it seems almost banal; but simple and inconspicuous facts of this kind can afford the clue to things of the greatest importance.

The fact in question is the extraordinarily high proportion of major classics in which there is a character who decisively preponderates over all the others: a character, one might almost say, for the sake of whom alone the other characters and their affairs are brought together. By no means every work is of this kind; but the interest of the case emerges more fully when we call to mind some of our current or classic formulations on the subject of what a great imaginative work *is*, and consider what proportion of works, on the basis of these formulations, we should expect to display this very distinctive feature. The answer is, that it is far from one which we should expect to prove especially sympathetic to the writer's purposes. Rather, if anything, the reverse. We should expect it to prove a somewhat difficult and recalcitrant literary form, as it were extreme and at a limit; and one therefore in which the examples of outstanding and classic success were few. If we think of Johnson's 'just representations of general nature', or Arnold's 'the application of ideas to life under the conditions of poetic truth and poetic beauty', or James's 'All life belongs to you . . . try and catch the colour of life itself', or Dr Leavis's 'a vital capacity for experience, a kind of reverent openness before life, and a marked moral intensity'; or if we recall a catch-phrase like 'the world of the novelist', or the idea touched on before, of the great literary work as suggesting in some implicit way what the world is like and what men are and how they should live, we find little or nothing to lead us to expect the feature which has been referred to, to be one frequently recurrent in literature; and a good deal, surely, to lead us to expect its infrequency. Yet, over and over again, it transpires that our major masterpieces, in many different languages, and in time from *The Odyssey* to *Ulysses*, take this seemingly improbable form.

Perhaps, indeed, the situation is a little stranger still. If I may be allowed to count a pair of lovers as a single unit (and this is no inordinate concession), the recurrence of this kind of work becomes even more noteworthy. More significant is something very distinctive about the rôle which the decisively preponderating character, in instance after instance, seems to take. It is a curiously ambivalent rôle, part victim and part cynosure, splendid and yet in a sense almost abject at once, the rôle of one who is passing through what is both an ordeal or infliction, and a triumph. This distinctive ambivalence, once it is noticed, seems to survive in treatments of the most varied kind. The distinctive stature, distinguished yet almost the opposite of that, is traceable in Odysseus, Aeneas, Dante, Gawain, most or perhaps all of the tragic heroes of Shakespeare, Clarissa Harlowe, Julien Sorel, Milly Theale, Isabel Archer, Tess, Bloom—the list may be extended almost indefinitely. It seems to invite a very distinctive response on the reader's or spectator's part; one that is travestied by speaking merely of our sympathy for the character, since it is a response by which we enter deeply and compassionately into his or her predicament or ordeal, yet at the same time realize that its interest and value to us lies in its very extremity, and are unwilling to have it in any way abridged or mitigated.

To some extent, it might be claimed, these features require no explanation. The sceptic might argue that the narrative which concentrates on one character is the simplest kind there is: it naturally occurs often and is often successful. Some of the things, he could go on, which befall such a character must of necessity be more favourable to him than others, and the ambivalent status of the principal referred to just now is little more than an elaboration of that straightforward and insignificant fact. If, however, to explain the facts away like this remains unconvincing—and surely it does—a very significant parallel emerges. Exactly the same distinctive feature is present in a high proportion of a society's major rituals; those not only of sacrifice or dedication, but also many rites of passage (marriage, initiation), and also all those in which there is a central ministrant to conduct a rite that is at once a severe challenge, demanding all or more than all his powers, and an opportunity for a personal triumph. Not all rituals have this distinctive feature, a conspicuously preponderating central figure; in view of which fact we might infer that if there is any genuine analogy between the imaginative work and the ritual, it may extend even more widely than this discussion is going to attempt to suggest. But the general situation is as follows. When we conduct a wideranging survey of works of imagination, we find that a notable proportion of them (especially of those which have become major classics) have a highly distinctive feature, steadily recurrent, and not explained, but rather the opposite, by the established accounts of what such works are doing. We are afforded a reason—one on such a scale that it seems to spread, as it were, right across the map—for thinking that great works of the literary imagination operate in a dimension which is unrecognized by, and if anything concealed by, the conventional accounts of them. If we turn to another field of behaviour, that of ritual, we find an activity which in a similar high proportion of cases displays this same very distinctive feature, for reasons which this time are much more obvious. We can find, also, certain further though less striking respects in which these two very different, and no doubt historically independent, forms of behaviour seem analogous (those which were touched on briefly at pp. 177–8 above). What is the correct inference to draw? Presumably, that there is at least one kind of literary work which, in some major respect though doubtless not in all respects, performs in our society, comparatively devoid of ritual as it is, social functions analogous to some of those performed by rituals in other societies; and furthermore that it can have this partial similarity in its functions because it is partly similar in its nature.

VI

Insofar as this train of thought is speculative and precarious, it is unattractive; in other respects it seems to be not so. It affords us a viewpoint from which the great imaginative masterpiece appears in a convincing perspective. Its irreplaceable value as part of the cultural heritage, its explosive and disturbing power, its total difference in kind from anything offered by cognitive thinking or in particular by science, its ability to contact the deepest parts of our nature, and the well-known fact that encountering it can be a decisive experience and mark a stage in our lives, now all fall easily into place. The answer, of course, is a partial one: the analogy with ritual is clearly incomplete. Much requires to be done by way of defining and limiting the argument, drawing distinctions, recognizing how imaginative works perform no one task but a variety of tasks, and elucidating how those which have most in common with rituals shade off into those which have less in common, or nothing in common at all. For all that, this train of thought seems to lead forward. It looks as if the great, the unique facts about imaginative masterpieces might come out along this road: not recede and be obscured.

A ritual is not a kind of statement. It is not admitted or denied or proved: it is something in which we take part. On the other hand, it is a distinctive sub-kind among the things which are objects primarily of participation. We could take part in a football-match, but the participation is of another kind, because of necessity there is no pre-arranged order, sequence or climax, and anything can happen at any time; whereas the essence of a ritual is to have a rigidly sequential order, one it may be which mounts to a climax in a recognizable rise and fall. We could take part in a military tattoo, in which there might well be a fixed and perhaps climactic sequence; but there is still a contrast with the ritual, for a tattoo will make narrow (if stringent) demands on our consciousness and our personality, whereas the demands of the ritual (they are also, in a sense, the possibilities which it opens for us) may be comprehensive. We could take part in an activity such as a communal fell-walk, which might have its fixed sequence and its climax, and might be comparatively comprehensive in what it offered and demanded. But one striking difference from any ritual would be that, wholly or in part, we might determine what we did in the course of it; whereas in the ritual this would not be so. Needless to say, ritual has other features, some of them perhaps more sharply distinctive of it.

The present train of thought seemed worthy of note because it seemed to throw light on the nature of works of the literary imagination. If the great work of literary art has come in part to offer us what the rituals of other societies have offered their members, and has come to do so through being in some respects the same kind of thing, from the present point of view it appears as in the first instance a source not of pleasure, not of insight (whether into fact or value), but of experience: an experience peculiarly comprehensive and demanding, an experience unified, ordered and imposed. This is perhaps the point at which it begins to transpire that seeing the great work as 'an imitation of life' or 'a criticism of life' is a little like contemplating an engine, and noticing all its parts, but not seeing that *it works*. What is seen is true and important, but that for which it is there has not been mentioned.

Or, to vary one's terms, it could be said that the central quality of a great imaginative work is to be not descriptive, not explanatory, not evaluative, but—the word will seem a strange one—'additive'. It is not merely a reflection or interpretation of other things, but a thing, offering a uniquely comprehensive and ordered experience of itself, in its own right. If—to employ a term which I used earlier—it seems to seek out those aspects of experience which have *mana*, it does so not in the first instance to draw our attention to them and their powers, but to generate its own unique power. The great imaginative work does indeed touch life at innumerable points, it does indeed open our minds to the deepest issues of life as it does to the variety of life's passions and life's sensations. If it suggests views (what man does not have these, and what man drawing on all he has but would have to deploy them?), these may have an immense interest, but in the end it will be an incidental interest. The work's essential interest will be to have added a great new item to the furniture of the world; to have become a thing, a fount of experience. It is precious to individuals because of the great experience which it offers them, and to society because, over centuries or over millennia, it thus enhances the life, and the capacity for life, of society's members.

NOTES

[1] G. Wilson Knight, *The Wheel of Fire* (1949 ed.), p. 73.
[2] D. J. Traversi, *An Approach to Shakespeare* (1956 ed.), p. 126.
[3] *The Age of Shakespeare*: Pelican *Guide to English Literature*, Vol. II (1955), p. 232; Cf. L. C. Knights, *Some Shakespearean Themes* (1959), p. 25.
[4] *Essays in Criticism*, Jan. 1958, p. 120.
[5] *Some Shakespearean Themes*, p. 24.
[6] *The Wheel of Fire*, pp. 80–1.
[7] E. M. Forster, *Aspects of the Novel* (1927), p. 41.
[8] F. R. Leavis, *The Great Tradition* (1950), p. 41.
[9] 'Coriolanus: Tragedy or Debate?'; *Essays in Criticism*, Jan. 1954, p. 18.
[10] S. L. Bithell, *Shakespeare and the Popular Dramatic Tradition* (1930), p. 130.
[11] *Some Shakespearean Themes*, p. 118.
[12] See, for example, Dorothy Osborne's *Letters to Sir William Temple*, *passim*; especially that of July 24th, 1653: 'Sure the whole world could never persuade me (unless a parent commanded it) to marry one that I had no esteem for'; and September 17th, 1654: 'if your father, out of humour, shall refuse to treat with such friends as I have, let them be what they will, it must end here; for though I was content to lose for your sake, them, and all the respect they had for me, yet, now I have done that, I'll never let them see I have so little interest in you and yours as not to prevail that my brother may be admitted to treat for me.'
[13] The following contemporary or near-contemporary illustrations of this great traditional commonplace may be of interest. 'Of ourselves we be crabtrees, that can bring forth no apples. We be of ourselves such earth as can bring forth but weeds, nettles, brambles, briars, cockle, and darnel.' (Second Part of the *Sermon of the Misery of Man* (Two Books of Homilies, 1859 ed., p. 20). 'Place not the expectations of great Happiness here below, or think to find Heaven on Earth; wherein we must be content with Embryon felicities, and fruitions of doubtful Faces' (Browne, *Christian Morals*, III. xi). 'Les grandes prosperités nous aveuglent, nous transportent, nous égarent, nous font oublier Dieu, nous-mêmes, et les sentiments de la foi. De là naissent des monstres de crimes, des raffinements de plaisir, des délicatesses d'orgueil, qui ne donnent que trop de fondement a ces térribles malédictions

Notes

que Jésus-Christ a prononcés dans son évangile: "Malheur à vous qui riez; malheur à vous qui êtes pleins et content du monde"! Au contraire, comme le christianisme a pris sa naissance de la croix, ce sont aussi les malheurs qui la fortifient. Là on expie ses pechés; là on épure ses intentions; là on transporte ses désirs de la terre au ciel; là on perd tout le goût du monde, et on cesse de s'appuyer sur soi-même et sur la prudence.' (Bossuet, *Oraison Funebre de la Reine de la Grande-Bretagne.*) 'Il ne faut pas avoir l'âme fort élevée pour comprendre qu'il n'y a point ici de satisfaction véritable et solide, que tous nos plaisirs ne sont que vanité, que nos maux sont infinis, et qu'enfin la mort qui nous ménace a chaque instant nous doit mettre dans peu d'années, et peut-être dans peu de jours dans un état eternel be bonheur, ou de malheur, ou d'anéantissement.' (Pascal, *Pensées.*)

[14] 'The powerful characters of the play all throw their weight against life— against the kind of love that Virgilia dares to stand up for, against the common pleasures of living which the citizens themselves point to' (*op. cit.*, p. 13).

[15] Cf. *King John*, IV. iii. 64; *King Lear*, I. ii. 170–3.

[16]
> Rightly to be great
> Is not to stir without great argument,
> But greatly to find quarrel in a straw,
> When honour's at the stake.
> (IV. iv. 54)

Cf. Castiglione, *The Courtier*, Book I: 'Neither let him run rashly into these combats, but when he must needes to save his estimation withall: for . . . he that goeth headlong to these thinges, and without urgent cause, deserveth great blame, although his chance be good. But when a man perceiveth that he is entred so far that hee cannot draw backe without burthen, hee must both in such thinges as hee hath to doe before the combate, and also in the combate, be utterly resolved with himselfe, and always show a readiness and a stomach.' Mr Traversi, writing that 'the two statements thus made (by Hamlet) have the appearance of a noble and consistent attitude based on "honour", but are actually in virtual contradiction' (*An Approach to Shakespeare*, 1956 ed., p. 101), seems not to recognize that Hamlet is uttering a traditional commonplace (nor to comprehend its soundness). The last sentence of the passage quoted from Castiglione bears plainly upon part of Polonius's advice to Laertes:

> Beware
> Of entrance to a quarrel; but, being in,
> Bear't that th' opposed may beware of thee.
> (I. iii. 65)

[17] Saxo Grammaticus, *Historia Danica*, Book III (transl. O. Elton, 1894, p. 117; italics mine).

[18] *The Wheel of Fire*, p. 20; *An Approach to Shakespeare*, p. 95.

[19] *Essay on Man*, I. 290; *Arcadia* (1590 ed.), Book III. Chapter 10.

[20] There is a good discussion of this point, in the context of *Antony and Cleopatra*, in P. Cruttwell, *The Shakespearean Moment* (1960 ed., pp. 126–30).

Notes

Castiglione, *The Boke of the Courtier*, IV (transl. Sir T. Hoby, Everyman Library ed., p. 288).

22 *Anatomy of Melancholy*, 3.3.1.2.

23 *An Approach to Shakespeare*, p. 142.

24 *The Common Pursuit* (1952), p. 139.

25 *Op. cit.*, p. 139.

26 *Anatomy of Melancholy*, 3.3.1.2.

27 *Explorations* (1946), p. 18.

28 *Anatomy of Melancholy*, 1.2.1.2.

29 Homily *Against Disobedience and Wilful Rebellion*, the Third Part (Homilies, 1859 ed., p. 572).

30 *Explorations*, p. 34.

31 Browne, *Religio Medici*, the First Part (*Works*, ed. G. Keynes, 1928, Vol. I, pp. 23–4).

32 See, e.g., E. Curtius, *European Literature and the Latin Middle Ages* (English ed., 1953), pp. 95 ff.

33 Hooker, *Laws of Ecclesiastical Polity*, I. iii. 2; Arnobius, *Adversus Gentes*, I. 2 (Anti-Nicene Christian Library, Vol. XIX, p. 5).

34 'Forðam on þisan earde waes, swa hit þincan maeg, nu fela geara unrihta fela and tealta getrywða aeghwaer mid mannum. Ne bearh nu foroft gesib gesibban þe ma þe fremdan, ne faeder his bearne, ne hwilum bearn his agenum faeder, ne broðor oðrum. . . . Forðam her syn on lande ungetrywda micle for Gode and for worulde; and eac her syn on earde on mistlice wisan hlafordswican manege . . .'. Wulfstan, *Sermo ad Anglos*.

35 Homily *Against Disobedience and Wilful Rebellion* (*ed cit.*, p. 574).

36 *Anatomy of Melancholy*, 3.2.5.5.

37 *King Lear* (Arden ed., by K. Muir, 1952, p. lxi).

38 *Piers Plowman*, C Text, IX. 203–222, and 229–231.

39 R. W. Chambers, *King Lear* (W. P. Ker Lecture: 1940), p. 44.

40 R. W. Chambers, *King Lear*, p. 43; L. C. Knights, *Some Shakespearean Themes*, p. 118; *The Wheel of Fire*, p. 206.

41 S. L. Bithell, *loc. cit.*; G. W. Knight, *The Imperial Theme* (1951 ed.), p. 324. Cf. p. 304: 'Cleopatra is all womankind, therefore all romantic vision, the origin of love, the origin of life.'

42 J. Danby, *Poets on Fortune's Hill* (1952), p. 149.

43 The idea of Antony's nobility is present here too, however, in the reference to the dolphin, the king of sea-creatures.

44 *An Approach to Shakespeare*, pp. 244–5.

45 Plutarch, *Life of Antony*.

46 The sense of the passage may be obscure in quotation. 'A Roman by a Roman / valiantly vanquished' is in contrast to what has gone before, and 'Roman' perhaps refers both times to Antony himself. Cf. IV. xiv. 61–2.

47 D. J. Enright, *op. cit.*

48 *Religio Medici*, the Second Part (*ed. cit.*, p. 73).

49 *Op. cit.*, p. 7.

50 For the association of these two ideas cf. H. Hubert and M. Maass, 'Essai sur Nature et la Fonction du Sacrifice', in *Mélanges d'Histoire des Religions* (1909), p. 81: 'Il ne serait pas tout a fait exact de se répresenter

86

l'expiation comme une élimination pure et simple. . . . La victime du sacrifice expiatoire . . . se charge d'une consécration qui n'est pas toujours différente de celle qu'elle prend dans les sacrifices de sacralisation. Aussi bien, nous verrons nous des rites de sacralisation et des expiatoires réunis dans un même sacrifice. La force que contient la victime est de nature complexe . . . c'est qu'en effet, comme l'a bien montré Robertson Smith, le pur et l'impur ne sont des contraires qui s'excluent.'

[51] E. O. James, *The Origins of Sacrifice* (1933), pp. 256–7.

[52] *Op. cit.*, p. 124.

[53] W. Robertson Smith, *The Religion of the Semites* (Third ed., 1927), pp. 84–8.

[54] D. H. Lawrence, *Letters* (ed. A. Huxley: 1956 ed., p. 190).

[55] E. Durkheim, *Les Formes Elementaires de la Vie Religieuse* (1912), p. 553.

[56] *Op. cit.*, p. 267.

[57] *Durkheim, op. cit.*, p. 529. A. Loisy, quoting this passage (*Essai sur le Sacrifice*, 1920, p. 95 n.: the reference to Durkheim is incorrectly given as p. 528) says that the observation is 'en contradiction avec des faits'. It should be noted that this expression of limited disagreement does not conflict with the restricted use made of Durkheim's suggestion in the present argument.

[58] *The Faerie Queene*, VI. viii. 46.

[59] Cf. J. G. Frazer, *The Golden Bough: Spirits of the Corn and of the Wild* (third ed., 1912), I, p. 248.

[60] A paper (somewhat revised here) read to the Colston Research Society Symposium on 'Metaphor and Symbol' at Bristol in 1960, and published in the Proceedings of the Twelfth Symposium of the Society.

[61] Cf. R. Otto, *The Idea of the Holy* (1917). In brief, Otto's argument is that holiness is not compounded of theological or moral convictions, but is the unique experience of a mysterious power and energy.

[62] Mr. J. M. Newton has drawn my attention to this passage.